THE STORY OF THE FIRST AMERICANS

BOOK ONE

ANCIENT TIMES

SUZANNE STRAUSS ART

The Fay School, Southborough, Massachusetts

PEMBLEWICK PRESS

Lincoln, Massachusetts

To Bob, With Love and Admiration

Acknowledgements

I am very grateful to my husband Bob, who carefully and painstakingly read and edited my early drafts. Teacher, writer, and editor in his own right, his criticisms of my writing are invariably perceptive, precise, and thought-provoking. Thank you, dear husband, for your unwavering and wholehearted support of all my projects. I'm also indebted to Allan Pineda, Fay parent and Mayan descendant, who read and commented upon my chapter on Mesoamerica. Special kudos go to Jesse Schacht and Bennett Wilson for their imaginative drawings of the man-eating Windigo. And, as always, I owe my inspiration to all my wonderfully curious and enthusiastic history students at Fay School. Honorable mention is unquestionably deserved by my patient and devoted writing companions — Darby, Bliss, Talbot, and Maude.

Other Books by the Same Author:
EARLY TIMES: THE STORY OF ANCIENT EGYPT
EARLY TIMES: THE STORY OF ANCIENT GREECE
EARLY TIMES: THE STORY OF ANCIENT ROME
EARLY TIMES: THE STORY OF THE MIDDLE AGES
WEST MEETS EAST: THE TRAVELS OF ALEXANDER THE GREAT
QUINTET: FIVE LIVELY PLAYS FOR KIDS
THE STORY OF THE RENAISSANCE

llustrations are by the author.

ISBN 0-9656557-7-6

TABLE OF CONTENTS

TO THE TEACHER

This is the first of two volumes about Native Americans written for students in grades five through eight. It begins with the first bands of nomads who crossed the land bridge from Asia during the last Ice Age and proceeds to describe how their descendants learned to adapt to a wide variety of natural environments. Each of the six chapters focuses upon a particular geographical region and traces the better known cultures that evolved there from earliest times until about the 12th century AD. Book II picks up the story and zeros in upon the lives of the natives inhabiting the American continents when the Europeans arrived in the 15th and 16th centuries.

I have taught American history for many years, and the topic of Native Americans has invariably sparked tremendous enthusiasm among my students. As a result, I have gradually expanded this unit in my curriculum, so that it now encompasses a great deal of material (which I cover in one term). My students eagerly delve into everything from ancient myths and petroglyphs to survival skills and the evolution of social hierarchies. They search for the answers to questions like "How do you build a massive pyramid without metal tools or labor unions?" and "Why were birds and snakes so important in primitive religions?" The subject matter is incredibly vast and fascinating, and new clues about the first Americans are being discovered every year. And yet, for a long time I was unable to find a basic text that covers the major cultures in sufficient depth without dampening the curiosity of a middle school reader. So I decided to write my own!

This book has the same tone and format as the other history texts I have written. The emphasis is upon the "story" element in history. After all, isn't history really a matter of how people dealt with varying circumstances and events, large and small, in different times and places? I have tried to keep the pace lively and to present an appropriate number of details (often "juicy" ones) to "bring history alive" for young students. Each chapter concludes with a set of review questions and suggestions for enrichment activities.

There is enough data in each chapter to give your students a solid understanding of the diversity of native cultures that flourished in ancient America and of the crucial role the environment plays in the forging of any society. But this is just the starting point. You should gather a large number of resource books from your school library. Happily, there are now available many lavishly illustrated volumes on Native Americans that portray "in living color" such marvels as the embroidery of Peruvian cloth, the intricate glyphs of Mayan stelae, and (via computer imagery) the reconstructed pyramid mounds of Cahokia. There are also abundant resources in other areas — computer software, videos, and musical CD's. (Native American flute music is a big seller in most music stores!) And, of course, there is the Internet.

Take your time with this unit, and give your students free rein to make connections between history and other disciplines (science, math, art, literature, music, even drama) and to compare the cultures of ancient America with other early civilizations of the world. (Mesoamerica and Egypt are "naturals" for a comparative study.) Most of all, have fun as you plunge into the very distant past of the American continents.

SETTING THE STAGE

Until this century, most historians regarded America as "the New World" — a place unknown and undiscovered until Christopher Columbus landed on an island in the Caribbean Sea. And yet, there were between 30 and 40 million people living on the American continents in 1492! The homeland of the American Indian covered one quarter of the world's habitable surface. How could anyone dismiss the presence of so many people thriving in this vast territory? Well, the Europeans *did* acknowledge the fact that there were "savages" living in America when they arrived. But they considered them barely human. To most Spanish and English explorers, the American natives seemed about as primitive as the monkeys screeching in the rainforest.

Is such a view justified? Of course, not! The natives that the Europeans first met were the descendants of people who came to the American continents thousands and thousands of years earlier. Their ancestors had learned to thrive in a wide variety of environments, many of them extremely challenging. And not only had they survived in their "new world," they created some of the richest cultures in the history of mankind. Savages, indeed!

Many people think that the only great cultures of ancient times sprang up in places like Greece, Rome, Egypt, and China. It's true, the people of these regions were among the superstars of the ancient world. But others living in America built a massive stone-faced pyramid centuries before the Egyptians built the famous Great Pyramid of Giza. There were bustling cities in America when the Romans were still living in mud huts. By the 5th century BC, when ancient Greece reached its "golden age," civilization was well established in many places on the American continents. Long before the Silk Road connected China with western Europe, merchants in Peru established an intricate web of trade routes linking towns in the mountains, deserts, and jungles of a big chunk of South America. This was just the beginning of what the ancient Americans would accomplish — and they did it all without the use of the wheel, metal tools, the horse, or the cow!

The first people to arrive on American soil looked at lot like the people who live today in eastern Asia. They certainly looked nothing like the apelike creatures who lived in Africa two million years ago from whom they (and you!) were descended. Actually, our species (*homo sapiens sapiens*— "thinking man") has been on the planet a relatively short period of time, a mere hundred thousand years! Our earliest ancestors learned how to survive in many different environments in Africa, Europe and Asia. They spoke a complex language, communicated their feelings through art, and carefully buried their dead for an afterlife. They fashioned a variety of stone tools for cutting and preparing meat, scraping hides, and chopping wood. (This is why those times are known as the Stone Age.) Their life was not an easy one. They spent most of their waking hours hunting animals and gathering plant foods just to stay alive. In fact, for 99% of the time man has lived on the earth he has had to forage in the wilderness for his dinner. Planting crops is something relatively new.

Life was difficult enough for those first humans, but they also had to deal with the inconvenience of living during an Ice Age. The era known by scientists as the Pleistocene Epoch (meaning the "most recent" Ice Age) began about two million years ago and ended as recently as 12,000 years ago. During that very, very long period of time, the northern polar ice cap repeatedly expanded and contracted. When it expanded, glaciers over a mile thick extended as far south as New York City and Berlin, Germany. The overall temperature of the planet was much lower than it is today. Just keeping warm was a challenge in itself in many regions. But the people living during those hard times were very resourceful. And they not only survived — they increased dramatically in numbers throughout Africa, Europe, and Asia.

> The Ice Ages were caused by slight changes in the orbit of the earth around the sun. Just a little difference in the orbit produces a huge change in the amount of heat reaching the earth.
>
> Why did the ice cap expand and contract? Because volcanic eruptions burst through the thick layers of ice, spewing ashes into the air and creating a very early version of the greenhouse effect. The planet warmed up and some of the ice melted. But when the ashes in the atmosphere dissipated, the planet got very cold again.

Finally, the world environment became more hospitable. The ice started to melt, and many parts of the planet became more livable. The end of the Pleistocene Epoch marked the dawn of something very special — humanity's taming of the American continents. It's a very exciting story, filled with action, adventure, and mystery. Interested? Then read on!

1 MAN ARRIVES IN AMERICA

Our story begins about 30,000 years ago. The long, long Ice Age was slowly coming to an end, although huge glaciers still covered great expanses of northern Europe, Siberia (in northeastern Asia), and North America. Along the southern edges of the glaciers stretched the desolate plains of the tundra. Although the tundra was inhabitable, it was not very inviting. Most of the year, savage winds and blasts of severe cold buffeted the frigid landscape. Only a thin layer of soil ever thawed out enough for scrub grass and moss to grow in the warmer summer months. And when it did, the melting snow formed ponds and marshes that were soon swarming with millions of mosquitoes.

South of the tundra, the environment became more hospitable to man and beast. Dense forests of fir and spruce covered the land and provided some protection against the howling wind and snow. Further south, the climate was more moderate, and vast grasslands stretched to the horizon, except where they ran into a mountain range. Compared to the bleak lands of the north, this lush region of gentle breezes, alive with a wide variety of plant and animal life, was a kind of paradise. Beyond it lay the equator, where the strong rays of the sun and the warm ocean currents produced a hot, steamy rainforest.

PEOPLE OF THE ICE AGE

About this time, human beings were more than holding their own in Africa, southern Europe, and Asia. Bands of families led a nomadic life, wandering from place to place in search of food. As the game animals moved on, the hunters were not far behind them, working as a team to stake out and kill their prey with their stone-headed spears. Meanwhile, the women and children gathered whatever plant foods they could find — nuts, berries, and edible roots.

Everyone dressed in the skins of the animals the hunters killed. The women sewed the skins together with needles made of bone threaded with animal sinews. (As you'll see, this would be the standard way of making clothes for many centuries to come.)

In the colder regions, the people wore several layers of skins to retain their body heat. They gathered wood to build fires to keep warm, to cook food, and to frighten away hungry predators. A few very observant tribesmen noticed the movement of the sun across the sky and devised a simple system for keeping track of time. They were history's first clock-watchers!

THE SIBERIAN HUNTERS

The people living on the Siberian tundra really had to use their ingenuity if they wanted to survive at all. Imagine a place where there are no trees, where the sun never even rises for many weeks in the winter, and where frost occurs even in summer! Although the winters were about nine degrees colder than they are there today, the air was much drier, and so there was not as much snow as you might expect. In some places, only a few inches covered the frozen ground.

The Siberians obtained most of their supply of food, as well as materials for clothing and tools, by hunting the wooly mammoth — a giant, hairy elephant-like creature towering twelve feet at the shoulders. (The largest mammoth species, known as the Imperial Mammoth, measured as much as 15 feet at the shoulders!) An average mammoth weighed over five tons and had curving tusks that were about eight feet long. The tusks were useful for sweeping ice and snow off clumps of grass and bushes. The

A Wooly Mammoth

mammoth was protected from the harsh weather by a very, very thick skin and three inches of insulating fat. Its undercoat of wool was covered with reddish brown shaggy hair that had long skirt-like fringes hanging nearly to the ground. Its broad pad-like feet were well adapted for walking through the snow, and they allowed the beast to lumber through the marshy pastures of the springtime tundra without getting bogged down in the mire.

It took some serious planning and a lot of courage to down a mammoth — and a bit of practical knowledge. The Siberian hunters noticed that the massive creature drank a lot of water (about 50 gallons a day), and so they would often hide behind some rocks near a waterhole until one turned up. Working as a team, they charged the unsuspecting animal as it waded into the shallow water. They stabbed it repeatedly with their sharp-pointed spears until it finally tired and weakened. Then they finished it off by plunging their weapons into the animal's heart and lungs.

> The remains of 40 frozen mammoths have been found in the frozen tundra, five of them almost complete. In 1977, the remains of a six- to eight-month-old baby mammoth, dating from 9,000 to 12,000 years ago, were discovered in northeastern Siberia. Apparently, his mother had been killed, and he had died of starvation. In his stomach was a bit of grass, remnants from his last meal. Archaeologists named him Dino and had him placed in a special climate-controlled case in a Russian museum, where he is viewed every day by interested visitors.

The hunters improved their odds against the huge, thick-skinned mammoth by using a spear thrower known as an *atlatl* (the name later given it by the Aztecs). This practical device consisted of a two- to three-feet long piece of wood with a handle at one end and a notch at the other. A hunter inserted the butt end

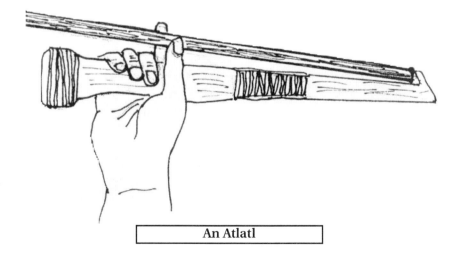

An Atlatl

of his spear into the notch, held the atlatl over his head, and then, with a swift, whip-like motion, hurled the weapon at his prey. The spear-thrower acted like an extra joint to his arm, enabling him to hurl his spear three times as far and three times as hard as he could with his bare hand. The atlatl was the first known tool made by humans to operate another tool. That makes it our earliest machine.

> A spearman wielding an atlatl was the equivalent of a modern baseball pitcher with a throwing arm that hangs down to his knees! Now that's power!

Once a mammoth had been killed, the hunters butchered its carcass with their stone axes. This, in itself, was quite a task, given the size of the beast, but it was certainly worth the effort. A single animal provided enough meat (up to 10,000 pounds!) to feed an entire band of hunters and their families for almost a year. The mammoth's heart (over a foot long) was regarded as a choice piece of meat, and it was often sliced and eaten raw immediately after the kill. After the carcass was cut up, the hunters dragged the pieces back to their huts.

Like the buffalo in later times, the mammoth provided most of the needs of the people who hunted it. The smaller bones were carved into tools and weapons, while the ribs and tusks formed the frameworks of their huts. The thick, wooly coat was used to cover these dwellings and was also fashioned into coats and blankets. And the dried dung fueled the hunters' fires.

BERINGIA

So much of the earth's water was locked up in the glaciers during the Ice Age that the level of the sea was often over 200 feet lower than it is today. As a result, large sections of the continental shelf stood above sea level, and many pieces of land were connected that are now separated by water. Think of the sandbars that appear near the beach during low tide.

Of greatest interest to us is the broad corridor of tundra that linked Siberia to Alaska. It is known as Beringia, after the Bering Sea that now covers it. This natural land bridge measured over 930 miles from north to south at its widest point and extended over 50 miles between Siberia and Alaska.

You've already learned how rugged the tundra could be in winter, especially with the long periods of darkness. Happily, in summer the sun stayed above the horizon for all but a few hours of the day. This brought to life a wide variety of plants and grasses, and these nourished the mammoth as well as the wooly-coated musk oxen, shaggy rhinos, giant bison, and herds of caribou. The animals grazed contentedly throughout the warmer months and stored up the energy-producing food that would get them through the long winters. But they had to keep a wary eye out for long-fanged carnivores like the dire wolf (twice as big as a modern timber wolf and equipped with bone-crunching jaws) and the saber-tooth tiger (which clutched its victims in its powerful claws and stabbed it to death with its eight-inch-long incisors).

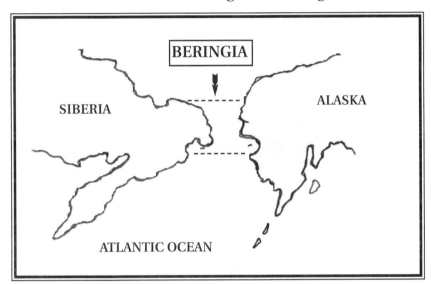

Sometime between 20,000 and 30,000 years ago, small bands of Siberian hunters began to follow migrating animals eastward into the Beringian tundra. They lived much as they had in Asia, seeking shelter from the cold in huts made from bones, tusks, and skins. They formed hunting parties to kill a larger animal or to ambush groups of the smaller caribou. They stockpiled most of the meat by burying it. This helped them survive the long winter. However, hunting wasn't always good. There were times when the food supply was so diminished that the old people would walk out into the cold to spare the others the burden of feeding them.

After the long dark winter, the hunters and their families moved on to a new camp, usually toward the east. (Beringia was a "two way street." Many animals traveled from America to Asia, and hunters often pursued them in that direction.) They supplemented their meat diet with seeds, berries, roots, and even insects. Those who ventured near the shore gathered mollusks and speared the fish that darted through the shallow waters.

Most people spent their entire lives in Beringia. It has been estimated that it took from 10 to 20 generations for one band of families to move across the land bridge. Certainly, no one had any sense of being involved in an historic migration from one continent to another. Everyone simply did what their parents had done — they made camps and then moved on when the animals did. But eventually there were human beings living on the North American continent.

The migration of the ancestors of most Native Americans across Beringia lasted several thousand years. Archaeologists (people who study prehistoric cultures) call the first American immigrants *Paleo-Indians*, which means "the oldest" or "most ancient Indians." Later migrations included the ancestors of the Apache, Navaho, and tribes of the Northwest Coast.

> When Christopher Columbus arrived in America, he thought he was in the East Indies, so he called the tribesmen he met there Indians. The name has stuck for all these years, but many people feel it should be permanently replaced by the term "Native Americans." What do you think?

Since they were Asian, it's not surprising that the first Americans resembled people living in the eastern part of that continent today. They were of medium stature and had straight black hair, light brown skin, prominent cheekbones, brown eyes, a broad nose with a low bridge, and little body hair. (Beards were unheard of!) The common tongue of the early hunters, known as *Amerind*, would evolve into nearly 2000 languages and dialects by the time Columbus arrived in America in the 15th century.

> Although the Paleo-Indians had little body hair, that which grew upon their heads was permanent. There has never been any such thing as a bald, full-blooded Native American!

In about 12,000 BC, the planet began to warm up. As the glaciers melted and retreated, the huge volume of water that had been bound up in the ice was released into the ocean, causing sea levels to rise. Little by little, the waters nibbled away at Beringia. Within a millennium or two, the land bridge had disappeared and the American continent was permanently cut off from Asia. Today, Beringia lies 120 feet below the surface of the Bering Strait. On a clear day, you can see the snow-capped mountains of Alaska from the Siberian coast 56 miles away.

But even after Beringia disappeared beneath the sea, groups of nomads continued to travel east from Asia. The ancestors of the Aleuts paddled across the water in small boats of driftwood covered with animal hides. They settled in the islands formed by the tops of the tallest mountains of Beringia. (They're known as the Aleutian Islands, taking their name, of course, from the Aleuts.) Meanwhile, the ancestors of the Inuit, also arriving by boat, set out across Alaska and Canada. You'll learn more about these rugged people of the frigid north in Chapter 6.

MOVING SOUTH

But let's return to those first immigrants. Once in America, most people continued to follow the animal herds south along a corridor of tundra that had opened up between two huge glaciers. Eventually, bands of hunters made it to the MacKenzie River in the dense forests of northwest Canada. This was an important achievement, because the river meandered south into the more temperate interior of the American continent. A variety of plants grew along the riverbanks, attracting many animals and providing some variety in diet for the hunters. Not that anyone considered himself a pioneer. As before, movement into new territories was a very slow process. Each generation progressed at a rate of only a few miles per year.

Fifteen hundred miles south of the MacKenzie River, the nomadic bands who made it that far entered the Great Plains — a vast grassland stretching southward from the present-day Dakotas for many hundreds of miles. During the following centuries, new generations fanned out across the continent. Some followed the river valleys east to the woodlands and the Atlantic coast, others ventured through narrow passes in the Rocky Mountains and then on to the Pacific, while many continued traveling south into Mexico and beyond. Still others would venture to the islands of the Caribbean Sea. And then there were those who liked what the Great Plains had to offer and simply stayed there. By 10,000 BC (a *mere* twelve thousand years ago) there were people living at the tip of South America – *Tierra del Fuego*. That was nearly 9,000 miles from Berengia!

Wherever they went, the new arrivals needed to constantly adapt and improvise, inventing new ways of life that were most suited to the wide range of environments in which they found themselves. You'll soon be learning about the cultures that eventually arose among the early Americans. But for now, let's take a closer look at those who remained on the Great Plains.

WHERE MOST CREATURES CAME IN EXTRA LARGE

Today the Great Plains consist of a vast swath of flatlands that cover our country's midsection. It's fairly arid in this region, especially the western parts, but at the end of the Ice Age the summers were cool and wet. This is because winds blowing off the glaciers to the north cooled the air and carried moisture south. The deeply rooted grasses and the many ponds and rivers of the Great Plains provided the ideal environment for all kinds of animals — most of them incredibly huge. In fact, 40 million of the largest game animals that have ever lived were roaming the Plains when the first people arrived there! It was a hunter's delight, provided the hunter wasn't intimidated by the great size of his prey.

> There were vast numbers of animals in America because they had few enemies. But why were they so big? Scientists propose it's because a bigger body is better able to conserve heat than a small one.

In addition to the mammoths and other beasts that you've already heard about, the Plains were home to beavers as big as bears (most were seven feet long, weighed 300 pounds, and were armed with eight-inch incisors!) and short-faced bears that were much larger than a modern grizzly. The American lion (much bigger than his modern African cousin) prowled about hungrily looking for dinner, as did panthers that rivaled the lion in size and ferocity.

> This is the only time that lions, tigers, and bears actually did live together. (Dorothy worried about them in well-loved classic, THE WIZARD OF OZ, fearfully chanting as she walked through the forest with her new friends, "lions and tigers and bears, oh my!")

The mastodon was an elephant-like mammal covered with coarse, reddish hair. It was smaller than a mammoth (even smaller than a modern elephant), and it preferred browsing in the shade of evergreen trees to grazing in the open. Another big grazing beast, the giant moose, had antlers spanning eight feet — or more!

A most peculiar creature was the giant ground sloth. It weighed in at three tons and was 20 feet tall when sitting down! And sitting was what a sloth usually did, using its muscular tail to steady its great bulk as it contentedly nibbled the tender shoots on the upper branches of tall junipers and pines. The sloth walked on the back sides of its front paws because its curved claws were so long that the soles of its feet could not touch the ground.

Another strange beast was the glyptodont, a clumsy, slow-moving mammal encased in a giant turtle-like shell. It weighed over a ton. Even the birds were huge — the ugly-looking teratorn (it resembled a vulture) had a wingspan of 15 feet.

Smaller animals of the Great Plains included the elk, the long-snouted tapir, deer, and peccary (a wild pig). And herds of camels and horses happily munched the tasty blades of grass.

A Giant Ground Sloth

There were so many creatures thriving on the bountiful grasslands that those eaten by predators made only a small dent in the general population. This would all change — dramatically — when man became the major hunter in America.

THE CLOVIS PEOPLE

For thousands of years, the descendants of the Beringians lived as their ancestors had done, moving from place to place in small family groups and using their traditional weapons and tools made of stone and bone to kill and process their prey. Those who inhabited the Great Plains flourished (no surprise, given the abundance of plant life and game!), and they increased in number. But it was never easy to kill a mammoth with the primitive spears that had been used for so many centuries, even with the aid of the atlatl. There was certainly room for improvement in the weapons department.

The tribesmen of one culture group, known to us as Clovis, met the need for better weapons by designing a new spear point. It made a big difference. The Clovis point was carefully chipped until the edges were extremely sharp. It was tapered (shaped something like a leaf), and it had a fluted central channel on one or both sides. The channel extended about a third of the way from the base to the tip and allowed the head to fit snugly into the notched end of the wooden shaft of a spear. The three to six-inch long stone point was lashed to the spear with animal sinews. By strengthening the connection between the spearhead and the shaft, the Clovis hunters produced a better and more dependable weapon. Think about it. Would you want to worry about the spear point falling off the shaft just as you aimed at an angry mammoth? The Clovis spear point certainly boosted a hunter's confidence. It was also America's first major technological breakthrough.

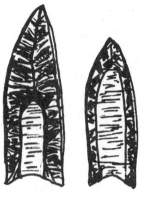

Clovis (left) and Folsom spearpoints

The name Clovis is derived from a town in New Mexico where, in about 9500 BC, a band of hunters left some of their distinctive spear points embedded in some mammoth bones. Apparently, they didn't cut off all the flesh of their prey and so they mistakenly left some of their points behind. Could they have been frightened away before they finished the job?

Similar points have been found in numerous sites in the Great Plains. Many of the Clovis points were cut from stones like obsidian, flint, and quartz. These stones are very hard and can be whittled into a very sharp point. Obsidian points were the best. The edges of this beautiful black stone, which is actually hardened volcanic ash, can be cut razor-sharp (so sharp a man can shave with it!). You'll be hearing a lot about obsidian — the steel of prehistoric times. Since these stones could only be obtained hundreds of miles from the site at which they were found, we know that the Clovis people either traded with other tribesmen or traveled great distances to obtain their raw materials. Quite possibly, they did both. But however they got the stones, their spearhead design was so much better than the earlier model that, over the centuries, it was being used by people living in nearly every part of the American continent.

In recent years, archaeologists have unearthed many remnants of the Clovis culture, and these help us to understand quite a bit about the lifestyle of those ancient people. We know that they lived in bands made up of from four to ten family groups. They worked together, hunting and foraging for food that was shared by everyone. They sought shelter in caves or skin-covered huts, and they often camped along rivers and long-vanished lakes (these dried up when the planet got warmer) so they could ambush the mammoths that came to drink. In addition to the spear points intended for big prey, they also carved some smaller points to hunt horses and camels, as well as birds, fish, and small game like rabbits.

> Carbon dating is a method of determining the age of living matter less than 50,000 years old. All living things absorb a known amount of carbon 14 from the atmosphere. When they die, the carbon begins to decay at a known rate. So scientists can measure the amount that's left to date it. The bones found with Clovis points were given the radio-carbon date of 9220 BC.

The Clovis people cooked their meat in shallow fire pits. (Archaeologists have discovered the charred bones of some of the beasts they consumed.) They also sun-dried some of the meat to preserve it for later consumption. The families augmented their diet by gathering whatever plant foods were available — mostly, as you'd expect, nuts, berries, fruits, seeds, and edible roots. But meat, and most particularly the mammoth, was their major source of food.

A number of buried bodies of Clovis people have been discovered in Montana. They were covered with ocher, a red clay-like material. No one knows why this was done, but perhaps it had some religious significance. As you'll see, many people who lived in later centuries did the same thing. We do know that the Clovis believed in an afterlife, since the bodies were surrounded with over 100 weapons and tools.

The Clovis culture died out on the Great Plains around 9000 BC, roughly the time when the mammoth and mastodon were becoming extinct. What caused the huge beasts to die out? Many scientists believe that they were over hunted. So when their numbers dwindled, the Clovis weapons and strategies were no longer practical. There are some good reasons for supporting this view. By that time, the numbers of human beings had grown dramatically on the American continent. Some simple math reveals just how much. If a band of 100 Beringians arriving in 10,000 BC could double their numbers with every generation, there would be half a million people in less than three centuries! Such a human population explosion would have had a massive impact on the wildlife.

But let's not forget that the climate was also changing. The earth was becoming warmer, and this, too, affected the animals — particularly the biggest ones. As the glaciers slowly retreated far to the north, the middle latitudes of North America became drier, with greater extremes of temperature in winter and summer. The grass of the Great Plains became shorter and tougher, and water spots grew scarcer. Massive herbivores like the mammoth simply couldn't find enough to eat and drink. This was a time when smaller, not bigger, was better.

THE FOLSOM PEOPLE

With the disappearance of the largest game animals, the surviving hunters of the Great Plains focused their energies upon the giant bison ("superbison"). This daunting creature resembled

the modern American buffalo somewhat but was a lot bigger. For starters, its curved horns were six feet long, and its massive body weighed about a ton! But it had a thin skin. Hunting the bison required a different kind of spear point, one smaller and more skillfully carved than the ones the Clovis had used against the mammoth.

A number of carefully made smaller flint points were discovered by a cowboy named George McJunkin among the bones of 23 giant bison in Folsom, New Mexico. They varied in length from one to three inches and were fluted with a wide channel that ran nearly all the way from the base to the tip, a feature that enabled the point to fit more firmly into the slotted end of the spear shaft than a Clovis point. Unlike the Clovis hunters, who shaped their points by pounding them, the Folsom tribesmen applied controlled pressure to the exact spot on the stone they wanted to mold. This enabled them to make a more delicate and refined weapon. Although spears bearing these points would have been useless against a thick-skinned mammoth, they were ideal for plunging into the flesh of a bison. (Look at the illustration of a Folsom spear point of page 10.)

The culture that produced these finer points is known as Folsom, after the town in New Mexico where the points were found. Like the Clovis, the Folsom people needed to trade or travel long distances to acquire their best materials — flint and obsidian. But it was well worth the effort. Points made out of other types of stone would have been less effective than those carved from these harder stones.

The Folsom hunters adopted a new strategy for downing their prey. Large numbers of men working together drove the bison into box canyons. (A canyon is a narrow valley with very steep sides. A box canyon has only one entrance.) Once the animals were trapped in the canyon, the hunters moved in for the kill. And they had other techniques. Sometimes they lighted grass fires and then amassed themselves along the lines of a wedge. Other strategically placed hunters shouted wildly to stampede the frightened animals into the point of the wedge, where they would be trapped.

After a kill, certain parts of the animal were set apart and even buried (not for later eating, but as a sign of respect). Probably this was done so that the animal's life force could return "home" to be reborn for another hunt. The hunters apparently believed that the beast willingly made itself available to them in exchange for this paying of homage. Variations of this mystical treatment of slain animals will turn up again and again in our study of early American cultures.

The bison provided a hunter's family with a huge supply of meat. A special delicacy was the creature's stomach, which was heated over a fire and then consumed along with its nourishing contents of partially digested grasses and other plants. Besides eating its flesh (and organs), the Folsom people used the bison's bones, horns, and teeth for tools, weapons and ornaments. They also used its hide, which they tanned (converting it into leather by soaking it with the animal's brains). The hide was fashioned into clothing, special ceremonial robes, and shelter coverings. And, as with the mammoth, the dung made excellent fuel for their fires.

THE PLANO PEOPLE

By 8000 BC, the Folsom culture had been replaced by another one known as the Plano. As with the Clovis, the disappearance of the Folsom people is best explained by the dying out of the major source of food — in this case, the giant bison. The Plano hunters pursued a smaller species of bison, known as the American buffalo. (This is the same animal that roams in certain national parks of the Great Plains today.) The climate continued to become hotter and drier in summer, and the smaller species were better able to survive on the dwindling amount of vegetation and water.

The warming of the planet had certainly produced some big changes. The hunter's paradise on the Great Plains was no more. By 6000 BC, two thirds of all varieties of animals weighing more than 100 pounds at maturity were extinct. And the disappearance of so many grass-eaters, in turn, brought about the doom of the fierce predators that fed upon them. More than 100 species of animals vanished from the face of the earth.

The horse and the camel met a different fate. Both species evolved in America millions of years ago. The herds of horses that crossed the land bridge into Asia were the ancestors of the modern horse. It's a good thing that so many of them traveled west, because not long after Beringia disappeared beneath the waves, the horses living in America were hunted to extinction. How different history would have been if the first Americans had learned to ride or harness the horse rather than eat it! Many camels also wandered into Asia. While those left behind in North America went the way of the horse, those that lived in the mountains of South America evolved into the modern llama and its close relatives. You'll learn more about them in Chapter 3.

Fortunately for many early Americans, the buffalo thrived for many centuries on the Great Plains. Their numbers were so great that they were not wiped out by the human hunters. (There were 30 million of them when the Europeans arrived!) To hunt the buffalo, the Plano, working in larger groups than the Folsom had, stampeded entire herds over steep cliffs. This strategy is known as the jump-kill. The first animals over the cliff were crushed under the weight of the followers, and the stragglers that survived the fall were done in by hunters waiting at the bottom with sharpened spears. A jump-kill could provide as many as 28 tons of meat, two tons of edible internal organs, and nearly three tons of fat, not to mention the hides, bones, and sinews. This was an early example of mass production!

> The Plano spear points lacked the fluting of the clovis and Folsom varieties. Actually, they were rather crude by comparison. Perhaps the jump kill made the spear points less important to the hunters.

The hunters butchered the buffalo on the site, first devouring the raw tongue. (Have you noticed that different cultures preferred to eat different parts of their prey raw? Would you prefer a raw mammoth heart or a raw buffalo tongue?) The most highly prized steaks came from the buffalo's hump. It was the tastiest and the most tender. The meat that wasn't eaten fresh was either cut into strips and sun-dried as jerky or preserved as pemmican. Pemmican was a long-lasting and nutritious food product made

> Even though the buffalo provided most of the needs of the Plano people, there were plenty of antelope grazing on the plains. These gentle creatures were often hunted for their soft skins as well as their tasty flesh.

by grinding up slices of jerky and mixing them with hot melted fat. (*Pemmi* means meat and *kon* is fat in the ancient tongue of the Plano.) Sometimes berries were added to the mixture for taste. The pemmican was packed in bags made from animal gut or hide and carried from place to place. Despite its rancid taste, this was America's first portable snack!

BEYOND THE PLAINS

While the hunters of the Plains learned to depend upon the buffalo to meet most of their daily needs, people living in other regions of America pursued smaller prey. Many made nets, traps and snares from plant fibers to catch rabbits, birds, and fish. Not that food was always scarce. Near the larger lakes, waterfowl were so numerous that they darkened the sky when they migrated. And the forests were teeming with beaver, bear, and more elusive creatures like the deer, elk, and moose.

Meanwhile, the idea of grinding the grains of wild plants into a coarse flour was beginning to catch on. Women learned to mix the flour with water and bake it over hot rocks to make bread. This innovation was more important than you think. The American diet was becoming much better balanced than that of the earlier hunters, who ate mostly meat. People were becoming healthier.

As wild plants and seeds took on greater importance, many of the nomads learned to weave baskets out of grass to carry them in. They even figured out how to make some of the baskets waterproof by lining them with clay. But they had no pots for cooking liquids. They certainly couldn't put a woven basket in the fire, so they did the next best thing. They boiled water *in* the baskets by dropping in stones or balls of clay that had been heated in the fire. Now they could cook stew and porridge.

The next important step was for the early Americans to learn how to grow their own crops. One of the first places that this happened was in Mexico, so in the next chapter we'll travel "south of the border."

REVIEW QUESTIONS

1. Can you describe the tundra?
2. How did the atlatl improve a hunter's chances against a mammoth?
3. What uses did the Siberian hunters make of the carcass of a mammoth?
4. Why was Beringia above sea level during the Ice Age?
5. Who were the Paleo-Indians?
6. How long (approximately) did it take for the first Americans to reach the southern tip of South America?
7. Why did Beringia disappear?
8. Describe three of the most interesting animals that lived on the Great Plains during the Ice Age.
9. What was so special about the Clovis spear point?
10. Why did the Folsom people design smaller spear points?
11. Why did the Folsom culture probably die out?
12. Why did so many species of animal become extinct?
13. Describe a "jump kill."
14. What was pemmican?
15. How did the people of the Great Plains make flour?

PROJECTS

1. Find out more about the huge time divisions of the early history of the earth. Here's some information to get started. The major periods (called eras) are the Paleozoic (beginning 600,000,000 years ago), the Mesozoic (beginning 225,000,000 years ago), and the Cenozoic (from 65,000,000 years ago to the present). These eras are divided into periods, such as the Jurassic (did you ever see the movie, "Jurassic Park?"). The periods are then divided into epochs, such as the Pleistocene. On a piece of poster board, make a graph showing the approximate time frame of these eras, periods, and epochs. Then indicate when the first mammals appeared on earth. Now show when the earliest forms of human beings occurred and indicate the period when modern man (homo sapiens sapiens)appeared on the scene. Finally, show how long people have depended upon agriculture to survive.

2. You've learned that during the Ice Age many huge animals lived in America. Their numbers were large because they had relatively few predators. But how can you explain their large size? Write a short report presenting your theory.

3. Make a model of a Clovis or Folsom spear point out of clay. When it has hardened, fit it into the notches you have cut in a piece of tree branch (your spear). Take some twine (representing animal sinew) to secure the point in the spear.

4. Write a report about a prehistoric animal of North America — the mammoth, mastodon, musk ox, giant ground sloth, giant bison, saber-tooth tiger, flat-faced bear, American camel, (prehistoric) American horse, or any others that interest you. Be sure to draw an illustration.

5. On poster board, draw a detailed map showing with arrows the movement of the first Americans across Beringia, down to the MacKenzie River, into the Great Plains, and beyond — all the way to the tip of South America.

7. In November, 1998, two girls from Derby, Vermont found a sharply pointed, dull gray two-inch stone with two short ears and a deep groove down the middle. For months the girls' families tried to discover the significance of the find. They wrote letters to everyone they could think of who knew anything about ancient America. It turned out that the spear point dated back more than 9,000 years. It is the oldest evidence of Native Americans in Vermont's Northeast Kingdom, and it proved that nomads wandered into Vermont's far north shortly after the glaciers retreated. Write a short play to reenact the discovery of the spear point and the events that followed. (Add humor and make it upbeat.) Perform the play with some friends for your classmates.

2 MESOAMERICA

Mesoamerica ("middle America") is a term used by archaeologists to describe the parts of Mexico and Central America that were civilized in ancient times. During the Ice Age, this was a region of grassy meadows and woodlands, but as the air became warmer, the inland areas were transformed into barren deserts. Large animals disappeared, leaving much smaller game like gophers, lizards, and even rats as prey for hungry predators. Moisture-loving plants were replaced by resilient desert species, like mesquite and cactus. Regions nearer the ocean continued to receive large amounts of rainfall and became steamy jungles.

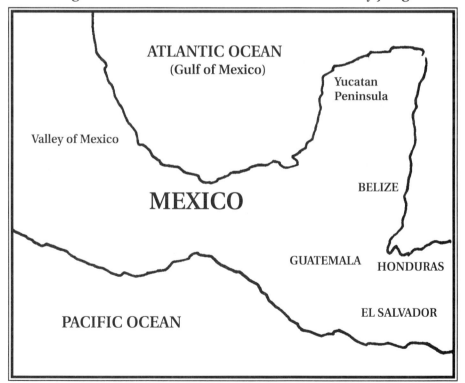

The first tribesmen who migrated into the highlands of Mesoamerica lived in caves and rock shelters. There was still plentiful game, which the men hunted with slings, spears, and blowguns, while the women and children collected plant foods.

But as the climate warmed, and even animals like the jackrabbit and antelope grew scarce, wild plants gradually became the most important part of the human diet. This would lead to a revolution that would change the lives of all Americans, sooner or later — the cultivation of crops.

BEGINNINGS OF FARMING

The earliest evidence of farming in Mesoamerica comes from the Tehuacan (Tay wah KAHN) Valley in Mexico. (It's also known as the Valley of Mexico). This was a natural basin set in a range of mountains and volcanoes. Measuring some 3,000 square miles and lying about 6,000 feet above sea level, it had once been covered by a large shallow lake. When the first people arrived there, a small part of the lake remained. (Today it's known as Lake Texcoco)

Around 5500 BC, someone living in the valley figured out that seeds would produce new plants if they were put in the ground and watered. It was probably a woman who made this discovery, since women did the cooking and most of the food gathering. Perhaps she accidentally dropped a few seeds she was gathering into some damp soil and then, returning to the same spot about a week later, noticed some new plants sprouting. If she was clever, she would have made the connection between seeds and plants. However it happened, this discovery had mind-boggling implications. For the valley dwellers, growing crops made it possible for large numbers of people to survive even though game was limited. And now, instead of searching for wild grains, families had a fairly dependable supply of food close to their campsite.

> The Mesoamericans were not the first farmers in the Americas. That distinction goes to settlers in Peru. You'll learn about them in the next chapter.

The first plants grown in Mesoamerica produced small, pumpkin-like squash. Eventually, the people learned to grow beans and avocados. Remains of some of the first crops grown were found buried beneath centuries of dirt and dust in the floors of caves, well preserved by the hot, dry conditions of the Mexican highlands. These early plants looked just like the wild ones. But, in time, certain wily farmers began to select only the largest seeds to sow the following year. This strategy produced bigger and more productive crops.

CORN, THE WONDER CROP

Squash, beans, and avocados are tasty and nutritious, but the best was yet to come. In about 5000 BC, the first corn was harvested in Mesoamerica. By modern standards, this crop was not very impressive-looking. It was a straggly plant, a variety of wild grass called *teosinte*. It produced cobs less than an inch long, each one bearing about a dozen tiny grains, or kernels, which were unprotected by any outer leaves. A number of small cobs found in the valley date from about this time. For a very long time (several thousand years!), these tiny cobs played a fairly small role in the diet of the tribesmen, merely supplementing the other plants they grew and gathered. Their major use was apparently for making beer!

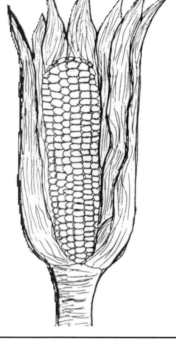

A Modern Ear of Corn

Eventually, corn evolved into a more substantial plant that produced multiple cobs. Each cob was now protected by a husk and had many rows of kernels. A single plant yielded hundreds of edible seeds. What a breakthrough! Now a harvest of corn could feed many more people than any other crop. A family could grow in 120 days twice as much corn as they could consume in a year. The new, improved variety of corn would become the major source of food in most of America for millennia to come!

As the farmers became more dependent upon corn, they came to regard it as a sacred food, even as a deity. After all, didn't their lives depend upon the harvested crops? Prayers were frequently offered to the recently planted fields.

Even today, more corn is grown in the United States than any other food crop. And modern ears of corn produce 200 times more grain than those first tiny cobs of Mesoamerica.

The ancient corn was prepared in many ways. The cobs could be roasted over the fire or cooked in boiling water. Most of the time, however, the women soaked the dried kernels overnight in a solution of lime or ashes to remove the tough outer skin. Then they washed away the solution and the skins and ground the kernels into flour, using a stone rolling pin (called a *mano*) and a flat stone slab (a *metate*). The flour, mixed with water, could be cooked as porridge or spread over a hot stone that had been heated in the fire to make tortillas (round corn pancakes that are still very popular in Mexico today).

Of course, a certain percentage of the kernels were stored to be eaten during the cooler months or to be planted the next season. At first, the women stored their kernels and other seeds in bowls carved from stone. Later, they learned to coil clay into the shapes of pots and other vessels. Pottery is too fragile to be carried around between campsites. The fact that so many pieces have been found dating from this early period provides further evidence that the people lived in permanent villages near their fields once corn became the staple of their diet.

By 1500 BC, the knowledge of how to grow corn and other vegetables (including tomatoes, pumpkins, and peanuts) had spread throughout the highlands and even to the coastal lowlands of Mexico. Men and women worked together planting and harvesting their crops. They even learned to grow cotton, which they used to make all sorts of useful items, including nets for hunting and, of course, clothing.

But it isn't easy to grow crops in regions that receive almost no summer rain. The farmers experimented to find the best method for bringing water to their plants until they hit upon something truly ingenious. Using sticks as shovels, they dug long canals to channel water from underground springs or nearby lakes to their fields. They were the first farmers in North America to irrigate their crops. (Irrigation refers to the process of diverting water from a source, like a spring or a river, to parched land in order to grow crops.)

Eventually, the settlers were able to produce more food than they needed. So now certain people could specialize in other tasks, such as weaving or making tools and pottery. Some, who sensed the presence of "other worldly" spirits more than others, devoted their time to learning to communicate with the nature gods. These priests, known as shamans (SHAH minz), would become very powerful in Mesoamerican society. You'll see.

By settling down in one place and dividing up the responsibilities of everyday living, the early communities had taken the first steps towards civilization. The term "civilization" refers to a society that has reached a high level of organization, technology, and artistic development. People who are hunters and gatherers don't have much time to think about these things, but those living in permanent villages with a guaranteed supply of food are better able to seek ways to improve the quality of their lives.

THE OLMECS

About 1200 BC, a culture known as the Olmecs created the first civilization in Mesoamerica. The Olmec heartland lay in the sweltering tropical lowlands and swamps along Mexico's Gulf Coast — about 350 miles east of the Tehuacan Valley. The Olmecs evolved from a group of farming settlements to a tightly organized society governed by an elite group of nobles. The rulers lived in a capital known as San Lorenzo. (Find San Lorenzo on the map on page 40.) The Olmecs traded extensively with neighboring peoples, and this helped to spread their beliefs and traditions into the Mexican highlands and even to the Pacific Coast.

San Lorenzo was, as far as we know, Mesoamerica's first great religious and political center. Built on a 165-foot plateau (a high, flattened land form) that rose above the Coatzacoalcos River, it could be seen for miles around. Its main feature was a large earthen mound, which was probably the base for a temple. The mound contained tens of thousands of cubic yards of earth, clay, and sand, every bit of which had been hauled in baskets by workers up the steep sides of the plateau. Imagine the labor required to perform this gigantic task and the management skills necessary to direct the workers. This is major evidence of the impressive organization and management of Olmec society.

> The word *Olmec* means "rubber people." The Olmecs were named by the Aztecs, who lived in Mexico long after they disappeared. They were known as rubber people because they used the sap of the rubber tree to make balls for their games.

Flanking the mound were courtyards and a special enclosure that was America's oldest known ball court. Clay figurines found at the site depict ball players in action. (We'll learn more about the Mesoamerican ball games later in our story.) In addition to the giant mound there were 200 smaller ones. These were bases upon which the nobles built their houses. Other mounds may have been the sites of additional temples. The people of San Lorenzo were supplied with fresh water by a series of buried stone channels that were linked to artificial reservoirs.

The Olmecs are most famous for their huge stone carvings of human heads, which are believed to portray their rulers. (The carvings seem like portraits of individual rulers because each has distinct features and facial expressions.) The rulers wear helmet-like headdresses. At least eight of the heads once stood around the central mound at San Lorenzo. One of them is over nine feet high and weighs more than 20 tons. If it were given a body, it would stand almost 50 feet tall!

Just as amazing as the size of the heads is the way in which they got to San Lorenzo in the first place. They were carved from basalt, and the nearest source of this kind of rock is 40 miles away through deep jungle in the Tuxtla Mountains. Archaeologists believe that the heads were carved at that site by sculptors using quartz chisels and wooden mallets. Then they were probably dragged on log rollers overland to the Coatzalcoalcos River and floated on large rafts downstream to San Lorenzo. It has been estimated that several hundred men were required to drag a 20-ton stone. Here's another example of Olmec teamwork! Artists painted the heads purple using a dye extracted from a mollusk that lived in waters off the Gulf Coast. Only traces of the coloring remain.

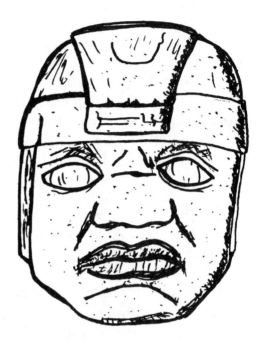

An Olmec Stone Carving of a Ruler

The massive heads were not the only examples of Olmec art. Craftsmen produced finely worked jade axes, figurines, and pendants. Pale green jade, the color of young corn, was considered a sacred stone. Actually, it later became the Mesoamerican symbol of wealth. Jade is an extremely hard stone. How could it be cut without the benefit of metal tools? Olmec craftsman discovered they could shape a stone using only a piece of string, some water and some sand. Sound impossible? Here's how it was done. The craftsman used the string as a saw, moving it back and forth over granules of wet sand placed on the jade. The constant seesaw motion slowly dug a groove, which he kept wet and sandy.

Archaeologists have also found Olmec carvings of strange and terrifying supernatural beings. Many resemble creatures of the jungle, such as the jaguar, snake, cayman (a relative of the alligator), and harpy eagle. Perhaps the most terrifying is the were-jaguar — a half human, half jaguar deity. It is often depicted as a chubby howling baby with sharp fangs and angry eyes. This creature — the offspring of a woman and a jaguar — was perhaps considered the Olmecs' ancestor. It was certainly widely worshipped. The jaguar itself was regarded as a mysterious and powerful creature of the hidden recesses of the earth. (It often crept stealthily through the jungle underbrush.) The Olmecs believed that this fearsome cat brought the rain and caused eclipses by swallowing the sun.

Most of the carved human figurines have long faces and downturned mouths. Apparently, the Olmecs really liked the look of an oblong face, perhaps because it resembled that of the were-jaguar.

There is evidence that some wealthy parents shaped the soft skulls of their infants by pressing them for long periods of time between two wooden boards!

Another fierce-looking deity was a feathered snake. Why a snake with feathers? It's important to think in terms of symbols. For primitive people, birds were often regarded as messengers of the spirits that lived in the heavens. A feather symbolizes a bird. The snake, on the other hand, slithers across the ground people walk on. It represents "this world," or perhaps the more frightening aspects of it. So the feathered serpent embodied both the spiritual and the natural worlds. Snakes often also symbolize regeneration, or eternal life. This is because when the snake sheds its old skin and emerges with a new one, it appears to have died and then been reborn. This is why the ancient Egyptians worshipped the snake. The feathered snake would become one of the most important deities in Mesoamerica. You'll be hearing about it again and again.

The Olmecs created a wide trade network to supply their craftsmen with raw materials. They imported almost a ton of obsidian from the highlands of Mexico and Guatemala, and they traveled to distant places in the south to obtain the much valued jade.

At its peak, San Lorenzo probably contained around 1,000 people — mostly rulers, nobles, priests, and skilled artisans. Thousands of ordinary people lived in farming hamlets on the plain below the plateau. They provided plenty of crops, particularly the corn, for the upper classes. But the elite were not content with a vegetable diet. They consumed large amounts of fish as well as turkey and dog meat. (Turkeys and dogs were raised for this purpose.) They were even known to consume an occasional human captive!

Life was good for the residents of San Lorenzo until around 900 BC, when the capital was violently destroyed. Did the peasants revolt? Did enemy tribesmen attack the city? No one knows. We do know that the stone heads were deliberately smashed and buried. Altars were cracked, and relief sculptures (figures carved so that they appear to stand out from a piece of stone) were shattered. No one knows why this happened.

> The giant heads of San Lorenzo were buried in piled ridges of earth and lay there for centuries as the jungle reclaimed the land. Much later, natural erosion caused a few of the heads to tumble out of the ridges and down into the valley below. People of modern times were amazed by sudden appearance of these impressive reminders of the ancient past.

After this disaster, La Ventra (50 miles away) replaced San Lorenzo as the Olmec political and religious center. It consisted of a group of pyramid-shaped earthen mounds and enclosures built on a tiny island in the swamps of northern Tabasco on the Gulf Coast. (Refer to the map on page 40 .) Most of the mounds were set around quadrangular plazas. The largest one (and one of the oldest) was over 100 feet high and 420 feet across. It was formed from tamped down earth (an unbelievable number of baskets of dirt had to be brought to the site) and was faced with clay. Today, it looks a lot like a volcano, with fluted sides and a conical shape. Archaeologists aren't certain of the purpose of this mound. Was it simply a giant copy of a volcanic mountain? (People in Mexico were awed, and terrified, by volcanoes — and for good reason!) A clue to its function lies in its alignment with the four points of the compass. The mound rises along a central road laid out precisely on a north-south axis. Was it used to measure the height

> Not everyone values the ancient structure of La Ventra. A complex that had survived for countless centuries to the north of the mound was destroyed in the 1960's when an airstrip was constructed on the site.

of the sun above the horizon at different times of the day? Was its purpose to measure time? We do know that the Olmecs created an extremely complex (and accurate) calendar, which was based upon their very precise observations of the heavens. But where did the mound fit in? No one is certain.

Some of the mounds of La Ventra were burial sites. Among the objects found there are finely chiseled axe heads, carefully carved necklaces, and figurines (most with jaguar features) cut from jade and other stones, including serpentine (a green stone of lesser quality than jade) and granite. Archaeologists have also found mirrors of magnetite (a magnetic iron ore). The priests wore the highly polished mirrors as pendants and used them to start fires in religious ceremonies by focusing the rays of the sun on piles of dry grass and twigs. La Ventra also boasts a set of huge basalt heads, similar to those of San Lorenzo. The stones were transported from a quarry 60 miles away.

Perhaps the most fascinating feature of La Ventra is a group of three pavements, each made up of 485 greenish serpentine blocks overlaid with mosaics of were-jaguar masks. These pose yet another mystery. Apparently, as soon as one layer was completed, it was immediately covered with dirt and another layer was arranged on top of it, which, in turn, was buried. No one can figure out why there are so many layers, or why each one was covered up by the next. Can you?

About 400 BC, La Venta met the same fate as San Lorenzo. It was destroyed and its monuments were brutally defaced. This marked the end of the Olmec domination of Mesoamerica. But they certainly deserve a special place in the prehistory of Mexico. Not only did they build massive mounds and carve impressive figures, they were also the first ancient Americans to develop a system of writing (a primitive form of picture writing) to record dates. That's how they were able to create their calendar (the first in the Americas). Unfortunately, most of their written symbols were carved into wood, which rotted away in the jungle moisture. How different our understanding of the Olmecs would have been if they had carved more of their messages on stone.

TEOTIHUACAN

About 30 miles northeast of modern Mexico City lie the ruins of Teotihuacan (tay oh tee wah KAHN). Built around 150 AD, Teotihuacan was not simply a ceremonial site like San Lorenzo or La Ventra, housing a small population of ruler, priests, and artists. Rather, it was a true city — the first planned city of America — with perhaps 200,000 inhabitants at its height (and even more people within its borders during religious festivals).

Teotihuacan was the commercial, cultural, and religious center of Mesoamerica for seven hundred years! It owed its success and prosperity to a strong centralized government led by a class of well educated priests. The city stood above the narrow, mountain-hemmed route between the highland valleys and the tropical lowlands of the Gulf Coast. This was a strategic location that guaranteed a wide trading market.

In the hills behind the city was one of Mexico's finest deposits of obsidian — that hard, brittle volcanic glass you've heard so much about. By the 6th century AD there were 350 obsidian workshops in Teotihuacan, employing thousands of people. This was big business, the heart of the city's economy. Merchants carried the obsidian tools and weapons as well as pottery, jewelry, and woven cotton cloth to distant regions. They exhanged these products for turquoise (in western Mexico), shells and incense (along the Pacific and Gulf coasts), jade (in Guatemala), and quetzal feathers, jaguar skins, and cacao beans (in the lowland jungles).

The Zapoteks were the successors of the Olmecs. By about 500 BC they had conquered most rival valley towns in Mexico's Oaxaca Valley, west of the Olmecs. Their city — Mount Alban — became the region's capital. Some people consider it the first true city in Mexico. The Zapoteks had systems of writing, calculation, and measurement of time based upon astronomical observations. They created a hieroglyphic script to record their history — a big improvement over the Olmec picture writing.

The glyphs carved on 140 stone slabs tell of the city's rise to glory. Among them are figures of men in contorted position s with open mouths and closed eyes. Several are bleeding, and some are mutilated. One is simply a severed head. These are the corpses of slain enemy chiefs or kings.

Mount Alban was built on a hill that had been leveled by laborers. It had many temples and pyramids, including 170 tombs of kings and the elite.

The city collapsed in about 700 AD. But despite the occupation of most of their territory, the Zapotecs survived as a people. Their language is still spoken. Benito Juarez, president of Mexico (1806-72) was a full blooded Zapotec.

Teotihuacan's nearly eight square miles (an area as large as early imperial Rome) were covered with towering pyramid-shaped mounds, palaces, apartment compounds, workshops, and marketplaces. (There were 2,600 major structures!) A system of canals brought water from underground springs to the nearby fields and also served as narrow waterways for transporting products.

The main road of the city was the straight, four-mile long Avenue of the Dead, running north to south through the center. It was 60 feet wide and lined with over 75 temples and the palace-like dwellings of the city's rich. A second wide avenue ran east and west, so the two roads divided Teotihuacan into four equal quadrants.

Huge apartment complexes of white stucco (something like cement) housed most of the population — over 100 people living in each one. Windowless outer walls buffered the noise from the streets and helped keep the rooms cool by day and warm by night. Instead of doors, curtains were hung from entryways to provide privacy. In each complex, the rooms surrounded a spacious patio that let in light and air and had drains to carry away rainwater. It must have been a pleasant place to live.

> The Aztecs, who lived long after the demise of Teotihuacan, gave the city the name by which it is now known. It means "place of the gods." The Aztecs believed this was where the gods were born and where they created the sun and the moon.
>
> The Aztecs named the main road the Avenue of the Dead, because they mistakenly believed that the pyramid temples were tombs.

Near the apartments were hundreds of workshops. Excavations have revealed that certain parts of the city were occupied by people of particular professions— tanners, potters, jade carvers, obsidian craftsmen (the majority, of course), and weavers lived together in sections in close proximity to their workshops.

The wealthy people of Teotihuacan lived in palatial homes with impressive stone pillars supporting the roofs. The inner walls were decorated with colorful fresco paintings of gods and mythological symbols. A fresco is painted on a wet plaster wall. As the plaster dries, it becomes part of the wall. This helps to preserve the painting. (If

> The potters of Teotihuacan mass-produced many of their pieces in reusable molds.

you've ever studied ancient Greece and Rome, you've probably noticed many similarities between the dwellings of the wealthy people of those cultures and the Teotihuacans.)

Archaeologists have found circular pits about a yard in diameter in the soil of the patios and even the floors of some of the rooms of the homes. These are graves containing bones, often half-charred, and pottery vases. Apparently, the people burned their dead. Buried with the remains were death masks modeled in clay and covered with pieces of turquoise or shells. Were these intended to identify the souls of the deceased when they entered the afterlife? Perhaps.

The Teotihuanacans ate huge quantities of corn. It was usually prepared as tortillas that were cooked over small braziers (ovens) made of clay. They even drank beverages made from corn. Meat dishes for special occasions included deer, rabbits, domesticated turkeys, and plump puppies (often cooked in honey). For desert there were figs and the fruits of the calabash and prickly-pear cactus.

Along The Avenue of the Dead

Let's take a closer look at the pyramids built along the city's main avenue. The largest and oldest, the Pyramid of the Sun, was a huge terraced structure with a flat top. It consisted of a series of square platforms of decreasing size built one upon another. The temple that once occupied its summit was reached by a series of grand stone staircases leading up the west face of the pyramid from the plaza below. You'll be seeing this design again in other parts of ancient America.

This Pyramid of the Sun was the religious center of the city, the sacred spot where priests conducted ceremonies in hopes of bringing about a good harvest, or some much needed of rain, or simply to make sure that the sun rose and set. The priests of Teohuanacan carefully studied the movements of the stars

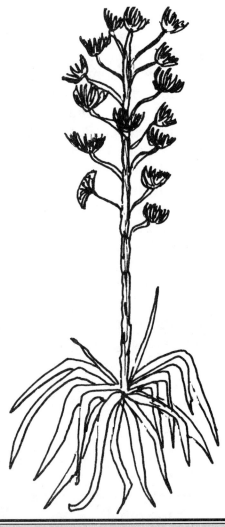

The maguey cactus grows very slowly. It doesn't even blossom until it is ten years old, and then it dies! (Luckily, suckers sprout from the base to form new plants.) Its leaves are up to six feet long, and the stalk can reach 40 feet. The cactus stores several quarts of liquid in its base, and this is often tapped by a thirsty desert traveler.

In ancient times, Mesoamericans sucked the juice out of the cactus base using reed straws. They stored it in gourd containers, where it fermented until it became pulque, a very powerful alcoholic beverage. The fibers of the leaves were used for making cords and as thread for clothing.

and planets, and they kept careful track of the seasons so that they could perform their rituals at the appropriate times.

Experts estimate that it would have taken a work force of thousands of laborers 50 years to build the Pyramid of the Sun. Its dimensions were truly amazing. The pyramid soared more than 200 feet above the Avenue of the Dead, the height of a 20-story building. Its base, measuring about 730 feet on each side, was almost equal to that of ancient Egypt's Great Pyramid (the world's largest pyramid). About 35 million cubic feet of stone and brick rubble made up its mass. The huge structure was faced with a layer of adobe bricks that were, in turn, covered with red volcanic rocks set in mortar. Originally, the pyramid had two other "skins" — another stone facing and a stucco coating — but these were blasted away at the beginning of the 20th century when the huge building was first being excavated. In those days, dynamite was commonly used to penetrate ancient structures! (Imagine the irreparable damage that was done!) The Pyramid of the Sun remained the largest man-made structure in North America until the 20th century.

THE PYRAMID OF THE SUN

Archaeologists believe that the design of the giant pyramid represented the Teotihuacan view of the universe. Its form embodied a number-sign that was sacred to most ancient peoples of Mesoamerica — the *quincunx*, which consists of four points set at the corners of a square, with a fifth point in the center. The central point symbolized the heart of life, the vital place where opposing forces met and became unified. In the case of the pyramid, the temple can be considered the fifth point in the center of the flattened structure rising from a square base.

> A large circular stone carving of a skull surrounded by a circle of rays found near the front of the pyramid is thought to symbolize the descent of the sun into the underworld at the end of the day.

Scholars also suggest that the pyramid represented a link between this world and the spirit world, since it was built over a volcanic cave. (Caves were considered sacred because they often held springs of cool, fresh water that flowed from deep within the earth — something of a miracle in a parched, barren land.) The cave has recently been excavated. Within it were found ancient burned offerings of fish and shells.

At the south end of the Avenue of the Dead was the Citadel, a sunken plaza surrounded by smaller platform temples. It might have once been the site of a royal palace. In the center of the plaza rose the elaborate seven-tiered Temple of Quetzalcoatl (kayts ahl koh AH tuhl), the Feathered Serpent. (Remember the feathered snake god of the Olmecs?) His snake-like body covered with the feathers of the quetzal bird, Quetzalcoatl was a god of water and fertility in Teotihuacan. He made the corn and other crops grow. Jutting out dramatically from the pyramid base were great stone heads of toothy serpents. These represent Quetzalcoatl and his opposites, the fire serpents associated with the desert (and death). Traces of the original red and green mineral paints can still be seen on the feathers. These weren't the only stone serpents in town. Adorning the facade of the temple was a series of sculpted serpent heads con-

Head of the Feathered Serpent

nected to the body of a single undulating feathered serpent. Deep beneath the steps of the pyramid were burial pits. These contained the bodies of sacrificial victims. Their arms were tucked behind their vertebrae and their wrists were crossed as if they had been tied.

> Sometimes the skin of a sacrificial victim was flayed (sliced off, like an animal hide, with a very sharp knife). These skins were apparently worn by priests to honor the gruesome skinless god, Xipe Totec ("the Flayed One").

The Feathered Serpent was clearly the major god, but another important deity was the rain god, Tlaloc. (Think about how crucial adequate rainfall was to the farmers in that hot, dry land.) Tlaloc was depicted with round, goggle-like eyes surrounded by many rings. He had long, protruding teeth — not a pretty sight, but probably symbolic of his power. (Remember the fanged deities of the Olmecs?) The steps of one of the temples lining the Avenue of the Dead were carved with the alternating heads of the Feathered Serpent and Tlaloc.

> In 1964 the Mexican government decided to move a monumental statue from Teotihuacan to a newly constructed museum in Mexico City. The statue, believed to be of Tlaloc, the rain god, had lain on its side for over a thousand years. It was 23 feet tall and weighed 168 tons!
>
> The villagers of the area, being highly superstitious, protested and tried to halt the action, but to no avail. The government then bribed them with promises of new roads, a new school, and electricity. (Promises which were kept.)
>
> The statue was loaded onto a huge flatbed truck. Then something truly amazing happened. Despite the fact that it was the dry season, the heavens opened up and it poured, not for a short time, but for many hours. Nearly everyone was convinced the rain god was offering his own protest!
>
> Today the statue can be viewed and admired in its new home, where it is protected from environmental pollution.

At the opposite end of the wide boulevard from the Citadel was Pyramid of the Moon. It resembled the Pyramid of the Sun but was built on a much smaller scale. Like the other great temples, it was a religious center, not only for the local people but also for pilgrims, who came from greater distances.

After centuries of prosperity, Teotihuacan unexplicably collapsed. Scholars have proposed a number of possible reasons for its demise, such as climatic changes (perhaps a long drought) or the exhaustion of the fields due to over planting. Or did the widespread deforestation of the region produce erosion of the countryside? Huge amounts of firewood were needed to burn the lime used to coat the city's pyramids and apartment complexes, and maybe overcutting of trees eroded the surrounding fields. Or did the city fall because the people were killed by a ravaging disease? Many buried remains reveal the presence of a serious disease. Was the city burned? We do know that in 750 AD a large area of the city was destroyed by fire. Were the people attacked by tribesmen from the north? Or did the populace feel drained by the massive building projects? We can speculate endlessly. Unfortunately, the people left behind no written records to offer clues about what happened. This is but another of history's mysteries.

THE MAYA

The greatest of ancient American civilizations was undoubtedly that of the Maya (MY uh). They benefited from the innovations of the Olmecs and Teotihuacans and then improved upon them. They also developed a rich tradition of religious beliefs and rituals, built fabulous temples, and produced some fantastic works of art. Best of all, they covered the surfaces of every stone building and marker they built with written accounts of important political and religious events. Thanks to the many records they left behind, we know quite a lot about them.

The ancestors of the Maya were probably nomads who arrived in Mexico around 3000 BC. When they learned to grow crops, many families settled in villages throughout the highlands of Mexico. Others settled somewhat later in the lowlands of Guatemala, Honduras, and southern Mexico — a region known as Peten (Pe TEN). By 1000 BC, many Mayan communities were well established in the highlands and lowlands. Between 400 BC and 250 AD, some of the villages expanded into good-sized cities. The Maya achieved their greatest heights (known as their Classical Period) between 250 and 900 AD. During this time, powerful kings ruled over 50 independent city-states throughout the dense jungles of Peten, making this region the heart of Mayan culture.

You might think it strange that people could achieve such great things in a steamy jungle. It certainly wasn't easy. Try to envision a rainforest of towering mahogany and ceiba trees —

their branches alive with brightly colored toucans and macaws and howling monkeys. Hungry jaguars prowl through the vines and undergrowth along the jungle floor, while deadly snakes slither silently around decomposing logs. The air is hot and humid, and buzzing insects are everywhere. This doesn't seem like a good place for farming, does it? But the Maya proved that it was. They cleared portions of land by hacking away the thick vines, felling trees, and burning the brush. They planted their seeds in the ground made fertile by the ashes, and in time they harvested a variety of vegetables — corn, beans, cassava, cucumbers, squash, peanuts, and chili peppers. As the population of Peten grew, new farming land was claimed by cutting a network of canals through the marsh and piling up the nutrient-rich muck from the canal beds. The newly made islands were extremely fertile, ideal for growing more crops.

The jaguar was the largest cat in the Americas. It was also the most powerful and most feared carnivore. It was a solidly built creature, measuring up to 9 feet (counting the tail) and weighing as much as 300 pounds. No wonder the native people of Mesoamerica considered it "larger than life." It frightened them, but they also admired its ferocity and courage. Today, the jaguar is in danger of extinction and survives only in undeveloped rainforests in Central and South America.

The Super Cities

Let's take a closer look at the Mayan city-states of the Classical Period. (A city-state consists of a central capital city and the surrounding area. Its territory might include hundreds of square miles.) As was the case in ancient Greece, the city-states of Peten shared a common cultural and religious heritage but never joined forces to form a single system of government. Each "min-kingdom" had its own ruler, who was advised by a small group of nobles (usually his close relatives). When a ruler died, his power was automatically passed on to his eldest son.

The Mayan kings claimed to be descended from the gods, and they had their divine ancestry inscribed on stone monuments and city walls. The people paid tribute to the king in the form of crops or labor (working on public building projects). The wealthy elite lived in luxury inside specially constructed ceremonial cities, while the majority of the population — the farmers — resided in small villages near their fields.

One of the most powerful Mayan city-states was Tikal (tee KAHL), situated at the base of the Yucatan Peninsula in the jungles of northeastern Guatemala. Its capital city was crowded with over 3,000 structures — temples, shrines, ball courts, plazas, reservoirs, palaces, and houses. The palaces were quite grand, consisting of groups of stone buildings with interconnected rooms and hallways, which were constructed on low platforms around open plazas. They were probably used as government

---

Many ancient Mesoamerican peoples played a unique ball game, known as *tlachtli*. The ball courts were usually located near temples. The playing field was shaped like an I, a narrow alley between sloping walls with two end zones. The ball, made of solid rubber, was very heavy and probably bounced really high. Two teams of seven players struggled to score a goal by hitting the ball through one of two stone hoops sticking out at right angles 18 feet above the stone floor of the court. A player could not use his hands or feet. He could only bounce the ball off his shoulders, hips, arms, or head. Players wore knee and elbow pads and special padding around waists to protect themselves. The game was actually a religious ritual. It was probably played between nobles of a city and high born warriors or rulers of a neighboring city who had been captured in raids. The losers (usually the captives) were often sacrificed as offering to the gods.

offices and as residences for the ruling nobility. Broad avenues linked different parts of the city.

Six of the temples were built on the summits of huge terraced pyramids. The Temple of the Great Jaguar towered 200 feet above the city. The pyramids were constructed from large amounts of rubble, covered with a thick layer of stucco and faced with limestone. In some cases, this outer casing was painted bright red. The temples atop the pyramids contained several narrow rooms and were richly carved with images of nature gods and of the deified Mayan royalty.

Tikal controlled a huge territory and stood at the center of an east-west trade route across the lowlands. Merchants and craftsmen brought great wealth to the city. At its height, Tikal had 80,000 inhabitants. After 889 AD, the city declined in power and was finally abandoned. Its monuments and temples were gradually overgrown by rain forest and lay hidden for almost a thousand years.

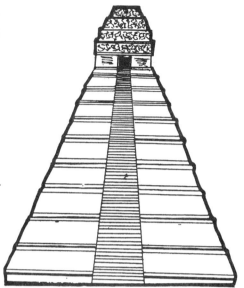

The Temple of the Great Jaguar in Tikal was featured by film producer George Lucas in his science fiction series, STAR WARS.

Copan (koh PAHN) was the most southern Mayan city-state, lying in a narrow valley in northwestern Honduras. It was very powerful in the 7th and 8th centuries AD. Its capital is famous for its stelae — upright stone columns carved with portraits of ruling families and hieroglyphic texts recording their rulers' history. (We'll learn more about the glyphs, or picture writing, later in this chapter.)

The steps of the immense Temple of the Hieroglyphs contain over 2,000 blocks carved with glyphs. They make up the longest piece of ancient writing in America. The steps were begun by Copan's greatest ruler, known as "18 Rabbit," to tell the history of his ancestors. This king with the funny name was a remarkable man — as well as a keen historian, he was a learned astronomer, avid city planner, nearly invincible warrior, and skilled athlete. Many of the stelae are carved with his portrait. He ruled

Unfortunately, about ten steps of the temple are missing, and many of those higher up slumped and tumbled through the centuries and were often put back out of place. With 70 per cent of the stones out of order, the long inscription makes little sense to us. Deciphering it is, of course, an on-going challenge for archaeologists.

proudly for 43 years, until he was ambushed and beheaded by warriors from the rival city of Quirigua.

Palenque (pah LAYNG kay) was the most westerly of the Mayan city-states, lying in southwestern Mexico. It was small and unimportant until 615 AD, when a new ruler named Pacal became king (at the age of only twelve). During his reign and those of his two sons, the city became large and powerful. (At one time, the supreme ruler of Palenque was a woman, something very unusual in the ancient world.) The sons of Pacal expanded his palace and added a graceful four-story tower, a structure seldom seen in Mayan architecture. The palace had its own water supply, brought from a nearby river via a stone-lined aqueduct. Stone carvings on the walls illustrate traditional ceremonies, such as the accessions of rulers.

The most interesting site in Palenque is the Temple of the Inscriptions, which stood atop a nine-tiered pyramid built by Pacal to house his own tomb. (According to Mayan mythology, the underworld had nine levels. Most archaeologists think the nine tiers of the pyramid represent this.) The temple's outer walls

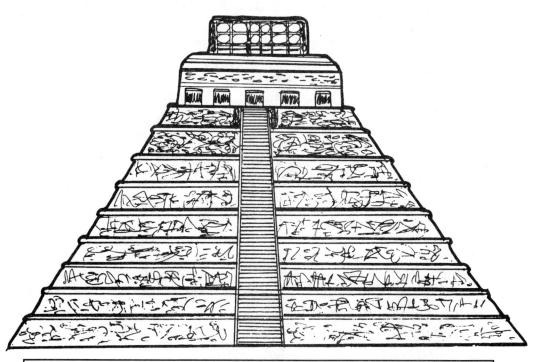

Temple of the Inscriptions

were decorated with carved images. Within its rooms were found three limestone tablets carved with long glyphic inscriptions. (This explains the name of the temple!)

Pacal was buried in a stone sarcophagus deep within the base of the pyramid. His tomb is reached by descending a stairway from the temple cut through the heart of the pyramid. Carved on the coffin are figures representing the ruler's ancestors and noting the dates of their deaths. A five-ton slab of limestone covering the sarcophagus is carved with relief figures. In the center is Pacal seated atop the setting sun but falling backward into the gaping jaws of a monster of the underworld. (Isn't this an eerie image?) From the center of his body grows the World Tree (more about this later), a sacred bird perched in its upper branches. Decorating the tomb walls are paintings of the nine Lords of the Night who ruled the underworld. Despite the extreme humidity of the ancient crypt, the figures are remarkably well preserved.

Imagine how excited the archaeologists must have been when they discovered all these striking clues about Mayan religious beliefs. They even encountered Pacal himself when they uncovered his skeleton within the stone tomb. It was adorned with jewelry made of gold and jade. His face was covered with a mosaic death mask made from 200 pieces of jade. The eyes were fashioned from white shells and obsidian.

After two centuries of great prosperity, Palenque weakened and collapsed around 800 AD. Its demise was soon followed by the fall of Tikal and Copan. The Classical Period of the Maya had come to an end, and most of the lowland cities were abandoned. No one knows exactly why this happened. Perhaps the ruling elite abused their power and caused rebellions on the part of the farmers, or perhaps the trading network fell apart. Maybe there wasn't enough food for a rapidly expanding population. Or perhaps the land simply wore out. Despite their many achievements, the Maya never thought about soil conservation. A strong possibility is that the cities were attacked by people living to the north. For whatever reason, the southern lowlands were abandoned.

But the story of the ancient Maya was not over. That rich culture continued to thrive in the northern Yucatan, thanks to the presence of yet another Mesoamerican culture, the Toltecs. You'll learn more about that period of Mayan history later in this chapter.

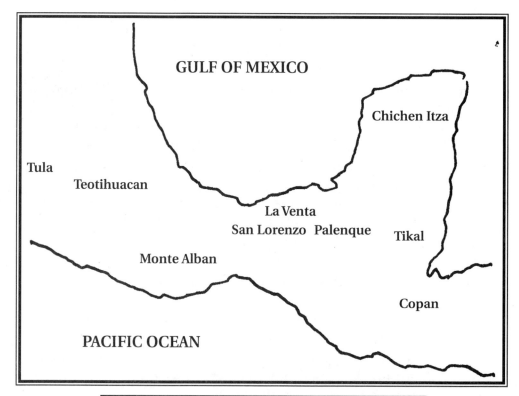

ANCIENT SITES IN MESOAMERICA

The Maya discovered chewing gum. They found that chicle, a thick, milky liquid that oozes out of cuts made in the wild sapodilla tree and then hardens into gum, was very tasty. Chewing gum has been enjoyed by forest dwellers of Mexico ever since . It was discovered by Thomas Adams in 1870 and, independently, a few years later, by William Wrigley, Jr.

Chewing gum became so popular in the United States at the beginning of the 20th century that natives of the Mayan region were pressed into service, seeking out more sapodilla trees. While searching for the trees they discovered the ruins of most of the great Mayan cities of the past that had been buried for centuries under the jungle growth!

The Daily Life of the Maya

Now that you've scene the big picture of Mayan history, let's take a closer look at the people themselves. We know from their art that they were short and stocky, with beak-like noses and full lips. Most had foreheads sloping straight back to a peak, looking rather like "cone-heads." They certainly weren't born this way! A typical Mayan mother periodically strapped her baby's head between two boards when the bones were soft, and the pressure molded them into a peak. (Do you think they got this idea from the Olmecs? They probably did.) Another sought after "look" was to be cross-eyed. (Oddly enough, the sun god was often portrayed with crossed eyes.) Again, the Mayan mother played the major role — she hung a toy or string of beads close to the baby's face so that every time he looked at them his eyes became slightly crossed. Would you like to be a cross-eyed cone-head? The Maya did!

The Maya wore light clothing that kept them cool and comfortable in the hot, tropical climate. A man usually donned only a cotton breechcloth (a strip of cloth tied around the hips and passed between the legs), while his wife wore a long cotton skirt and short overblouse. Body tattoos were very popular, the more the better, and on the days of religious festivals, the married men painted their faces red. (Boys and unmarried men covered theirs with black paint.)

Noblemen wore brightly embroidered or feathered cloaks and lavish jewelry — bracelets, necklaces, and anklets of gold, silver, and jade. The height of

The rare quetzal bird, prized for its glittering emerald-green tail feathers, lives in the moist rainforests from southern Mexico to Panama. Females are 14 inches long from bill to base of tail, but the tail feathers of the male can be three feet long. In early times, only Mayan nobles and priests could wear the plumes of the quetzal, usually on headdresses, armor, and capes — death was decreed for anyone else who possessed them!

The quetzal is the national bird of modern Guatemala.

fashion was to have jewelry dangling from the ears, nose, and lower lip, and even to have semiprecious stones set in the teeth! (Many of the elite had their teeth ground to a point, giving them the appearance of a hungry jaguar!)

The Mayan carvings portray the rulers (and the gods) wearing extremely elaborate (and heavy-looking) headdresses, adorned with the beautiful plumes of the quetzal bird. Most likely no one wore anything quite as cumbersome — Mayan art, like that of many other ancient peoples, often exaggerated certain articles of attire to emphasize rank and power.

The nobles lived comfortably in fine stone palaces, some several stories high. They were often carried about in city streets in elaborated decorated litters carried on the shoulders of their servants or slaves. The common people lived in simple houses of woven sticks plastered over with mud and roofed with thatched palm leaves. Many of these were built on earthen platforms raised above the marshes. The furniture consisted of a few hammocks. Most of the people lived near their farms, but they gathered in the cities to go to the market or attend religious events.

> The slaves of the Maya were men from rival cities captured in battle. Sometimes they were neighbors! When a Mayan citizen committed a serious crime, his sentence was slaverye (In cases of murder, however, the sentence was death.)

Corn made up 80% of the Mayan diet. Like other people you've read about, they ate their corn raw or ground it up and baked it on a hot stone. Tortillas were often served with honey (the Maya raised a species of stingless bees for this purpose) or filled with mashed beans, crushed peppers, fried fish, or ground meat (duck, venison, turkey, or peccary). Corn was the base for an alcoholic drink called *balche*, which was sweetened with honey and spiced with tree bark.

Cacao (kuh KAH oh) beans were roasted, ground, and mixed with corn flour. Small cakes of this paste were mixed with water and vanilla and shaken in a gourd to make a frothy drink — Mayan chocolate milk! It was drunk in one gulp during special religious rituals. Rich people stored the drink in special screw-top pots. Cacao beans were also used as currency. Dishonest merchants would strip off the husks of the beans and fill them with sand, mixing these fakes in with genuine beans. Wary customers learned to squeeze each bean before paying up!

The cacao tree is a thick-trunked evergreen that grows as high as 25 feet. Its fruit is a pod that looks a lot like a melon, measuring up to 12 inches from tip to tip. The pods grow on short stems close to the trunk. The seeds (the cacao beans) are embedded in the pod and are about the size of a lima bean.

On the Mayan market, a pumpkin was worth four cacao beans, a rabbit ten, and a slave could be bought for 100.

The Mayan Religion

The Maya believed that all things in the universe — people, animals, plants, and objects — had a spirit and were closely connected. The earth itself, they thought, was the back of a giant turtle that lived in a gigantic lake covered with water lilies. Below was the watery underworld, *Xibalba* (shee bahl BAH). It was divided, as you've learned, into nine layers. The heavens consisted of 13 layers.

The Maya recognized the four directions of the compass. Each was represented by a color and ruled over by a god. (East was red, west was black, north was white, and south was yellow. Why do you think they chose these colors?) East was the most important quadrant, or direction, because the sun rose there every morning. The four sides of a Mayan temple, often mounted by four stairways, reflect the four quadrants of the world.

Everything in the Mayan universe was bound together by a giant blue-green tree, called the World Tree. Its branches reached up into the heavens and its roots stretched down into the underworld, connecting the land of human beings with the invisible realms of spirits and gods. A sacred

The Maya believed that every person had an animal companion spirit. When he was born, a soul was placed in his body, and an identical soul was placed in the body of an animal. The fates of the person and the animal were bound together throughout their lives. Whatever happened to one happened to the other.

They also believed that people could transform themselves into their animal companion spirits during war or in dreams. Bloodletting also allowed people to conjure up their animal companion spirits. The companion spirit of the king was — no surprise here — the jaguar. To show his connection, he wore a jaguar helmet and a jaguar skin shirt when he led his men into battle.

bird sat among the tree's upper branches, ever alert to carry messages between earth and the heavens. (This was the tree — and the bird — sculpted on Pacal's tomb.)

There were over 50 Mayan gods and goddesses, and each was considered a vital part of a single supreme spiritual force. Itzamna was, for a long time, the most important of all the deities. He was the lord of the heavens and the god of day and night. He was also considered the god of medicine and the inventor of writing. You might expect such an important deity to look attractive, but Itzamna was usually portrayed as a cayman or a toothless old man with a hooked nose! Ix Chel, the moon goddess, was the wife of Itzamna. She appeared as an old woman. Ix Chel was also associated with healing, childbirth, weaving, and foretelling the future. All other gods were the offspring of Itzamna and Ix Chel.

Yum Kaax, the Corn God (from a carving)

Because rain was so essential for growing corn, Chac, the rain god, was a very important deity. He was often portrayed with a reptile face, a long snout, catfish-like whiskers, curved fangs, and body scales. Sometimes he appeared as a weeping warrior, his tears raining down on the earth. He carried an ax made of lightning.

Yum Kaax (yoom KAHSH) was the corn god. He was depicted as a handsome young man — an ear of corn often sprouted from his head as part of his elaborate headdress. Kinich-Ahau (kin EESH ah HOW) was the god of the face of the sun. All day he journeyed across the sky. When the sun set in the west, he descended into the underworld, changed into a fearsome jaguar, and passed through many dangers. At dawn, always victorious, he resumed his daytime identity and began his next journey through the heavens. (The ancient Egyptian sun god, Ra, also traveled across the sky by day and through a hazardous underworld by night.)

Twelve scary gods of death, war, and disease dwelled in the underworld. (Xibalda means "place of fright"). They were usually pictured wearing ornaments made of the disembodied eyes stolen from the dead and dying. The death god Yum Cimil had an ugly bloated body, skeletal face, and thin limbs. Ixtab, the goddess of suicide, was portrayed hanging from a tree, her body partially decomposed!

When a Mayan died, his body was painted red, and his mouth was filled with ground corn and cacao beans (to use as food and money in the afterlife). The corpse was wrapped in a cotton shroud and buried under the floor of the house where the person had lived. Other family members would later be buried beside it. When the floor of the house was full of bodies, the family moved out and the dwelling became a shrine to their ancestors. Of course, rulers and important people had grand funerals, and they were buried in stone tombs. Often their servants were killed and buried with them — to serve them in the afterlife.

> The tall kapok tree (also called the silk-cotton tree) is a relative of the baobab tree of tropical Africa. It has a thick, spongy trunk that absorbs water in the dry season, just as a cactus does.
>
> In the rainy season leaves appear, as do seed pods that are lined with silky fibers. The Maya gathered the fibers when the pods burst and used them to stuff pillows and even mattresses.

The souls of most people passed on to the underworld. Only the spirits of warriors and royalty went to a heavenly paradise, shaded by a giant kapok tree. Traveling to Xibalda was not an easy journey. To reach the deepest (and most pleasant) level, known as *Mictlan*, a soul had to make it through many hazards, such as turbulent waters, clashing mountains, and jabbing obsidian blades. The Maya believed that dogs were able guides for getting through these hazards, and for this reason the family pet was often killed upon the death of his master and buried with him.

The Mayan ruler was also the head priest. He performed rituals to appease the gods, thus assuring a good harvest while maintaining the world harmony. As we saw with Pacal, the ruler

> Like many other people of Mesoamerica, the Maya believed that the mountains connected the earth and the sky. The pyramid was simply a man-made mountain. Caves were believed to link the earth with the underworld, so the doorway into the temple on top of the pyramid represented the entrance of the cave — and therefore the entrance to the world of the gods. Of course, the great height of the pyramid made the temple itself seem very distant and almost a part of the heavens, just as the builders of the structure had intended.

was identified with the World Tree and represented the point of intersection between the natural and supernatural worlds. He and the other priests performed most of their ceremonies in front of a pyramid temple. At the appointed time, they would dramatically mount the pyramid steps, to the dramatic sound of drumbeats and horn blasts, while the people watched from below with wide eyes.

An important part of the Mayan religion was blood-letting. The people needed rain for their crops, so in exchange for this valuable liquid, they offered the gods blood from their own bodies. (As you've learned, tears also symbolized falling rain.) The ruler and his family set an example for everyone else. They ritually pierced parts of their bodies to sanctify major events — such as the birth of an heir, or a military victory — as well as to appease the gods on behalf of their subjects.

Blood-letting could be a painful process. It was usually done by pulling a thorn-lined string across the tongue, letting the blood drop onto pieces of bark paper. The paper was immediately burned in the hearth, so that the blood-tinged smoke could be consumed by the gods. Ordinary people drew blood by lancing their earlobes. They often wiped drops of their blood on statues of the gods.

Sacrifice was another way to appeal to the spirits. Usually animals — deer, dogs, and turkeys — were led to an altar where their throats were slit. Some of the blood was collected in special receptacles. But for special occasions — such as the crowning of a new king or the dedication of a temple — only a human sacrifice would do. In fact, the primary purpose of war among the Maya was to acquire captives for sacrifice. (Captured kings, however, were often kept alive for repeated bloodletting, since their blood was considered more pure than that of most people.) Surprisingly, the victims were treated quite well on their last day of life — their every wish was granted

Blood-letting through the tongue (From a carving)

(except, of course, the wish for freedom!). At the appointed hour, the victim mounted the pyramid steps accompanied by the priests, who were donned in jaguar skins with their bodies painted black. When the procession reached the top, the victim was forced to stretch out on his back upon a stone altar. With a quick movement of his hand, a priest cut out his heart with an obsidian knife. He lifted it, still beating, above his head, as the people below watched in wonder. Surely, eveyone hoped, this gesture would impress the gods!

Adventures in Math and Science

As you can see, the Mayan priests were very important and highly respected people. Every Mayan firmly believed that his very life depended upon the ability of these men to communicate with the gods. The priests also made offerings and said prayers to the sun, moon, and stars, since the heavens provided the earth with light and rain. Anyone who spends a lot of time gazing at the heavens is bound to notice that the stars and planets move in regular and predictable ways. These movements are linked with the seasons of the year. The Mayan priests saw the connection between the configuration of heavenly bodies and the seasons, and they used their observations to predict when the rainy season was due. This was very important, since it enabled the farmers to harvest their crops before the fields became waterlogged. The priests could even predict solar and lunar eclipses, and they were familiar with the cycles of Venus.

To record their observations, the priests devised a system of numbers using combinations of bars and dots. A dot represented the number one, a bar stood for five, and a cacao bean shell stood for zero. With these symbols they could write any number.

The Maya were the first known people in the world to devise the concept of zero and to use it as a place marker when writing their numbers. Our number system depends upon the use of zero. Think about it. How could you write the number 250 if you didn't have a zero to hold the place of the ones (units)?

We count by tens, but the Maya counted by 20's, probably because they first learned to count by using both their fingers and toes. Since they used a base of 20, the place value in their numbers went up by twenties. So the first and lowest place had a value of one, the next a value of twenty, and the next four hundred. In a written Mayan number, the place value increased from bottom to top, not from right to left as ours does. So while we read a number, beginning with the highest place value, from left to right (like 472), the Maya read their numbers from top to bottom (with the symbol for 400 at the top of a three-figure column).

> Europeans first learned about place value and the concept of zero in the Middle Ages, when Islamic scholars helped spread the knowledge of systems of math developed centuries earlier in India and China.

The Mayan numerical system was more flexible than the cumbersome numbers devised by the mighty Romans and used in Europe until medieval times. Mayan priests made computations in the millions! Some archaeologists have suggested that the Maya needed to perform complex calculations with very large numbers because of the smallness and cheapness of their money unit, the cacao bean. If this is so, one of the most important developments in mathematics was inspired by the humble seed whose shell was used to represent zero!

The priests depended upon their knowledge of math to design their huge monuments, but mostly they used it to calculate and record dates. The Maya were certainly not the first Americans to design a calendar — in fact, they based many of their calculations upon the one used by the Olmecs — but theirs was amazingly accurate. Actually, they had two calendars (a solar calendar and a sacred calendar), and, as you'll see, the two related to one another in some very important ways.

The solar calendar had 365 days, which were divided into 18 months of 20 days each, with an extra five days at the end of the year. (The Maya considered these five days extremely unlucky and spent most of that time fasting and making sacrifices to the gods.) A day was called a *kin*, a month was a *uinal*, and a year was a *tun*. The solar calendar was used for predicting astronomical occurrences like solar eclipses as well as scheduling the best times for planting and harvesting crops. It was quite accurate, although it didn't account for the additional quarter of a day required for the earth to revolve around the sun.

The sacred calendar consisted of 260 days, divided into 13 weeks of 20 days. Each day had a name associated with a god (one god for each of the 20 days) and a number, which referred to the week of the year. Examples of sacred dates are 1 Akbal, 2 Kan, and 3 Chicchan. When a child was born, the god representing that day became his patron deity. The solar calendar had a similar design, although, of course, it had more names and numbers.

The dots and dashes we learned about earlier were numerals (like "3") used in calculations. The Maya wrote number words (like "three") in picture symbols we call glyphs.

These were very detailed images of animals, people, and items from daily life. Each glyph represented a certain word or phonetic sound. The number words made up only a small fraction of the Mayan glyphs. There were over 800 of them, and they formed the most complex writing system in ancient America. You'll learn more about them later in this chapter.

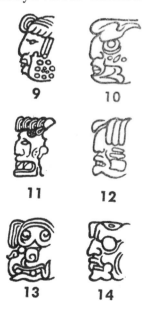

But let's get back to the two calendars. The numbers and glyphs were carved or written on large circles with pointed edges. The circles were placed side by side, the points of one locking into the grooves of the other. (Try to envision two meshed wheels, like the gears of a machine.) Each day the wheels turned one point. The current day was marked by the place where the two calendars were linked. So each day had two names — one from the solar calendar and one from the sacred calendar. This movement and linking of dates from the two calendars created cycles known as a Calendar Round. The priests studied the combination of gods and numbers of the calendars to predict good or bad luck.

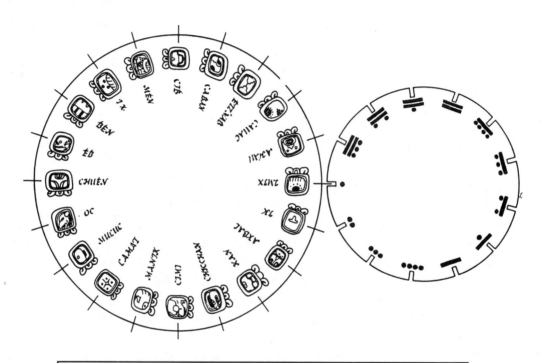

THE SOLAR CALENDAR (left) AND THE SACRED CALENDAR
(This is a simplified drawing. The actual calendars contained many more glyphs.)

Since the circles were of different sizes (the solar calendar being larger than the sacred one), the alignment of a particular day, such as 8 Ahau (the sacred name) 12 Ceh (the solar name) would occur only once in 52 years. When this happened, a cycle of combined dates (one Calendar Round) ended and a new one began. As you might expect, the occasion was marked by a great celebration — something like our welcoming in the new year, but much more exciting.

The Maya thought about the world in terms of millennia, and they developed a long term system of counting time, known as the Maya Long Count. It extended back to the day the universe supposedly began — August 13, 3114 BC by the modern Gregorian calendar. They counted ahead from that date into eternity. A given date was calculated by counting up the number of days that had elapsed since the fixed starting point. In addition to the *kin* (day), *uinal* (month), and *tun* (year), the priests calculated longer time frames — the *katun* (20 years) and the *baktun* (400 years). So the Long Count measured not only days of the year but vast cycles of time. (Notice how time was counted with a base of 20.)

Typical Glyphs

The Mayan priests preserved their knowledge of political and religious events by carving glyphs on rows of free-standing stone pillars called stelae (STEE lee), like the ones in Copan. Every five years they had a new one shaped and carved with glyphs to describe the latest happenings. Hundreds of glyphic inscriptions appear on the walls of monuments, too. In recent years, scholars have learned to translate about 80% of them.

The Maya also made paper from the bark of the wild fig tree. To do this they cut a piece of bark and soaked it in water until the fibers separated. Then they pounded it. A piece of bark that had been eight inches wide could be pounded until it stretched to six feet! Once the pounding was done, the bark was cut into strips and folded to make accordian-like books. These held official records and astronomical tables.

The Maya even experimented with printing multiple copies by cutting glyphs in reverse on blocks of wood the way modern printer's type is made. When the glyph was painted with dye and pressed against paper, it left a stamp.

> Fortunately, the Maya also recorded their history and religion on ceramic vessels. Thousands of ceramic vessels, covered with glyphs and portraits of gods and monarchs, have been retrieved from burial sites.

Hundreds and perhaps thousands of books were written about Mayan history, myths, and the simplest events of everyday life. Sadly, only four have survived. Three of these were sent to Europe by Spanish colonists, where they were preserved. The fourth was discovered in a cave in Mexico. All four contain astronomical information that was used to predict eclipses and determine days of good and bad luck. What happened to the other books? In some cases, the bark simply crumbled in the humid tropical weather. But most were destroyed by the Spanish explorers and settlers who arrived in America in the 15th and 16th centuries. (They considered them the writings of the devil!)

Much of what we know about Mayan beliefs is taken from three sources that were written down after the European conquest of Mexico by members of several Mayan tribes. The Chilam Balams, from the Yucatan, are a series of books that include songs, prophecies, historical events and details of ceremonies that were performed by the ancient Maya. The Annals of the Cakchiquels tell the legendary history of the Cakchiquels. The Popul Vuh (POH pole VOO) is a collection of legend, mythology, history, and astronomy. It was written in the 16th century by the Quiche Maya of Guatemala. Its title means "Book of the Community." Many consider it the Bible of Mayan beliefs.

The deciphering of historical glyphs began in 1958, when Heinrich Berlin proposed that certain commonly appearing glyphs identified a place or its ruling dynasty. At about the same time, Titiana Proskouriakoff, a renowned epigraphist (a scholar who studies inscriptions) proposed that particular inscriptions described important events in the rulers' lives. Following these leads, other scholars proved that inscriptions announced the lineage and accomplishments of kings and queens of several great cities. This opened up the door to translating many of the other writings.

The Sacred Tales

Two of the stories of the Popul Vuh explain how the world was created and tell of the adventures of the legendary ancestors of the Maya, the Hero Twins. These stories were well known by countless generations of Maya, and they provide further clues about their rich religious traditions. Here's a short summary.

Before the earth came to be, there was only sky. Then two gods— the Plumed Serpent (him again!) and Heart of the Sky (also called Hurricane) began to talk. Their words formed the earth and its mountains, trees, and plants. Then they made the animals — birds, jaguars, snakes, and smaller creatures. The gods asked the animals to praise them, but the animals just squawked and howled. So they made people, hoping that they would know how to worship them.

The first person was made from clay. His words made no sense, and his body was so weak that it crumbled. So the gods tried again, this time making people of wood. The wooden people spoke and had children, but they were ignorant creatures without souls. Even worse, they showed no respect for the gods, so they were conveniently destroyed by a great flood. A few were allowed to remain — today they live in the trees as monkeys.

Now the gods ordered that white and yellow corn be brought to them from the mountains. They ground the kernels nine times (have you noticed how often that number crops up in Mayan mythology?) and made the flesh of the first four true men, using water to create the human blood. These men were wise, and they understood how to worship the gods. But now the gods worried that their creations were too much like themselves! They clouded the mens' eyes so that they could see only what was nearby. To make up for taking away perfect vision and understanding, the gods gave the men beautiful wives. These early men and women were the ancestors of the Mayan people.

> A Spanish bishop, Diego de Landa, burned large numbers of Mayan books, saying they were the work of the devil. Fortunately, he later wrote his own book about them, and it is one of the most important sources of information about that culture.

The Hero Twins were human beings with god-like powers who, according to Mayan myth, rid the world of demons and made it safer for people born after them. Their names were Hunahpu (hoo nah POOH), which means Hunter, and Xbalanque (sh bah LAHN kay), meaning Jaguar Deer. Their father and uncle, also twins, had been ballplayers who were killed by the death gods of the underworld (Xibalba). (Losing in a ball game, remember, often meant death.) The twins grew up to be ballplayers, and they, too, went to Xibalba to compete with the death gods.

The death gods hoped the twins would not make it through the hazards of the Underworld, but they cleverly proceeded unscathed down Trembling Canyon, past the River of Blood and the River of Scorpions, through the House of Gloom and other dangerous houses until, in the House of Bats, Hanahpu's head was bitten off by a bat. Things looked bad for the twins, but Xbalanque made his brother a temporary head from a squash and, most magically, Hanahpu could again see and speak.

Finally, the twins played ball with the gods. (The gods used Hanahpu's real head as the ball, but Xbalanque tricked them and got the head back.) The twins knew the death gods would not be satisfied until they died, so they purposefully lost the game and allowed themselves to be sacrificed. The gods, ecstatic with joy, ground their bones and threw them into a river. But the twins were reborn as fish-men and returned to Xibalba.

Now disguised as poor actors, they danced and performed magic for the death gods. The gods, doubting the power of their magic, told them to sacrifice a dog and bring it back to life, which they did. Then the twins sacrificed a man and brought him back to life. As a final act, Xbalanque cut off Hanahpu's head and then brought him back to life. The death gods were extremely impressed (wouldn't you be?), and they foolishly asked the twins to kill *them* — and then, of course, bring them back to life. The twins gladly killed the death gods, but they didn't bring them back to life!

This is how the Hero Twins triumphed over the powers of death. After their great feat, they rose into the heavens, where they became the sun and the moon. For the Maya, the twins' victory against the death gods was symbolized by the daily setting of the sun (when it went into Xibalba) and its triumph over the forces of darkness (when it rose again in the morning). The moon reflected the stunning triumph of the sun.

When a Mayan king died, he, like the twins, went to Xibalda and triumphed over the gods of death. Then he rose to heavens, to be worshipped as a god. And when the Mayan nobles and warriors played ball, they believed they were acting out the scene from this myth. In this way, they identified with the legendary Hero Twins.

> The earliest members of the human species appeared on the earth about a million years ago. Once modern man learned to write (about five thousand ago in western Asia), prehistory ended and history began. That happened relatively recently. Just think. Prehistoric man lived by hunting and gathering for a period about two hundred times as long he has been able to write down his thoughts.

CHICHEN

We learned earlier how the great cities of Peten declined. When this happened, other Mayan cities in the northern lowlands of the Yucatan peninsula continued to thrive for some time.

The most important of these was Chichen (Chee CHAYN) which, about 700 AD, was a very large religious center. Pilgrims traveled there from distant places to cast offerings into the *cenote*, a huge natural well (180 feet wide) in the limestone that was sacred to the rain god, Chac. (Chichen means "mouth of the well.") The walls surrounding the well had fallen in over the centuries and the vine-covered sides were nearly vertical. The surface of the water, green with algae, was 65 feet below the top. The water was 30 feet deep. Throngs of pilgrims visited the well to honor the rain god. Occasionally, people were sacrificed to him. After their legs and hands were bound, they were tossed from above. Their bodies made a big splash and then disappeared.

Like other ancient cities you've been learning about, Chichen had its share of fabulous temples and palaces. The local priests devoted much of their time to studying the heavens. They even built an observatory — a round temple topped with a small room that had window-like openings in its thick walls. The window facing west lined up perfectly with the setting sun on the vernal (spring) equinox. But despite its grandeur, Chichen, like the more southern Mayan cities, was in decline in the 10th century. Fortunately, its fall was put off by two centuries because of the actions of some very unlikely allies, the Toltecs.

THE BLOODTHIRSTY TOLTECS

The Toltecs were a warlike people who subjugated a large part of ancient Mexico. They owed their power to their trading monopoly of obsidian in central Mexico. (Remember, obsidian was the "steel" of ancient Mesoamerica — an incredibly valuable material, especially for warriors who needed sharp weapons.)

The Toltec capital, Tula, was built on a high ridge about 40 miles northwest of modern Mexico City. At its center was a huge four-tiered pyramid whose temple was entered through a doorway flanked by stone pillars in the form of (yes, you guessed it!) Feathered Serpents! Tula had a legendary leader, Quetzalcoatl ("Feathered Serpent"), whose symbol was the open jaw of a snake with the golden-green plumes of the quetzal bird. (Isn't it amazing how often this image appears in Mesoamerican cultures?) In the mythology of the Toltecs, it is not clear whether he was a man before a god or a god before a man. But he became, as the story goes, the Toltec leader. And the temple atop the huge pyramid was his. The roof of the temple was supported by four huge stone columns carved as warriors. The base of the pyramid was decorated with armed warriors, wild beasts, and eagles devouring human hearts. The Toltecs had a taste for blood!

Symbols of death and military force turned up everywhere in the grim and joyless art of the city. A 60-foot long Serpent Wall within the city depicts snakes devouring human beings, much of the flesh already stripped from their skulls and bones. Stone racks held the skulls of sacrificed victims, while reclining figures (called Chac Mools) cradled basins on their abdomens — receptacles for human hearts! Walls and columns were covered with carvings of warriors, skulls and crossbones, serpents swallowing skeletons, and, of course, snarling jaguars. This was a grisly place!

In AD 1168, Tula was attacked — perhaps by fierce nomads from the northern desert. The temples and palaces were looted and burned, the Serpent Wall toppled, and the great stone warriors methodically smashed. The inhabitants fled, leaving Tula deserted and in ruins. Many of them ended up in the Yucatan.

Mayan myth tells of a Toltec warrior who arrived in Yucatan from the west. His name was Kukulcan (the Mayan term for "Feathered Serpent"). He conquered the peninsula and set up his capital at Chichen. Because he was aided by the Itza, a Mayan people from the Gulf Coast, the city was renamed

A Warrior Column

Chichen Itza (Chee Chayne EET sah). It represented a blending of Toltec and Mayan culture. This is when Kukulcan became the major Mayan deity, replacing Itzamna.

CHICHEN ITZA

Chichen Itza dominated northern Yucatan during the 11th and 12th centuries. It was a most impressive city. The most dramatic building was a temple pyramid, which the Spanish called the *Castillo* (once again, the Spanish invaders couldn't tell the difference between a castle and a temple). It stood in the center of the main plaza and was dedicated to Kukulcan. The pyramid was built in nine tiers (yes, nine!) with a staircase on each side. (Archaeologists have discovered that it was built over an earlier temple pyramid. Some scholars think the first pyramid was a royal burial site.)

The pyramid also served as a type of giant calendar. Each of the staircases had ninety-one steps which, added to the top platform, equal 365 — the number of days in a solar year. The staircases were designed to resemble the bodies of slithering snakes, whose heads rested at the foot of the pyramid. (Even the columns of the temple were shaped like serpents.) A shadow cast by the setting sun fell along the edges of the northern and eastern staircases every March 21 and September 21 (the days of the vernal and autumn equinoxes). Aren't you amazed by the Mayas' understanding of astronomy?

The nearby Temple of the Warriors was another colossal tiered pyramid topped by an impressive stone temple. On two sides stretched colonnades of 1,000 stone pillars supporting wooden roofs to shade the visiting pilgrims from the hot sun.

Chichen Itza had the largest ball court in Mesoamerica. It was 160 yards long and 40 yards wide, about the size of a modern football field. Carvings around its walls depicted members of the winning team cutting off the heads of their defeated opponents. Near the field was a long platform carved on all sides with human skulls impaled on stakes! (Remember, the Toltecs had a thirst for blood!)

A causeway led from the central plaza of the city to the sacred cenote. Pilgrimages to this well continued for centuries. Offerings dredged from its depths include incense, carved jade, and gold discs carved with battle scenes. Archaeologists have also discovered the bones of 13 men, 8 women, and 21 children.

> Sadly, trafficking of Mayan artifacts is big business today. Perhaps 1,000 pieces of fine pottery leave the region of Peten each month! Most sought after are ceramics of the late classic period (600-900), black line on cream pottery depicting mythological and historical events. Looters are paid between $200 and $500 per vessel, and collectors pay over $100,000 for the same pieces in a gallery or auction!

In the late 12th century, the ruler of a northern city (Mayapan) led a revolt leading to the sack of Chichen Itza. The marvelous city was destroyed, and Mayapan became the new capital of the Yucatan region. The Itza fled south to Lake Peten (now known as Lake Peten Itza), where their descendants lived independently and happily — until 1697, when they were attacked by Spanish soldiers. Despite the destruction of Chichen Itza, pilgrims continued to flock to the cenote until fairly recent times.

LOOKING BACK AND AHEAD

For a very long time, most of the fabulous Mayan cities lay buried beneath a mass of jungle vines. In 1839, writer John Lloyd Stephens and artist Frederick Catherwood rode mules along along muddy trails deep into the thick Central American rainforest in search of ancient ruins. Cutting through vines and branches with machetes, they discovered several abandoned cities that had been hidden for so many centuries. While curious monkeys chattered noisily from the trees, Catherwood stood ankle-deep in mud and sketched the huge carved pyramids and temples. He was somewhat encumbered by the gloves he wore as protection against the mosquitoes.

Stephens' four books about his and Catherwood's discoveries became best sellers, fascinating the world with tales of a mysterious civilization lost in the steamy jungles. Since that time, archaeologists have excavated dozens of monuments and temples covered with glyphs and discovered many tombs filled with ancient treasures.

In recent years, an explosion of interest in the ancient Maya has led to major new finds. And still, much is waiting to be discovered. About 3,500 sites have been found, yet only a few have been fully investigated. Meanwhile, about 2.5 million people, mainly living in the Guatemalan highlands and northern Yucatan, still speak Mayan languages. Many still revere the ancient gods, although Christianity has altered many of the native beliefs and practices.

REVIEW QUESTIONS
1. Where is Mesoamerica?
2. What were the first corn plants like?
3. Why is corn considered a "wonder crop?"
4. What does "civilization" mean?
5. What clues tell us that Olmec society was highly organized?
6. Describe the Olmec carved heads.

7. What was a were-jaguar?

8. What was the meaning of a feathered snake?

9. What is the greatest mystery about La Ventra?

10. Who were the Zapoteks and what's so special about them?

11. What was the basic layout of Teotihuacan?

12. How big was the Pyramid of the Sun?

13. What is the quincunx, and what does it have to do with pyramids?

14. Who was Tlaloc?

15. Give three reasons why the Mayan civilization is considered the greatest one in ancient America.

16. What were the three Mayan supercities?

17. Describe the Mesoamerican ball game.

18. What happened to Mayan culture after Palenque fell?

19. Describe the Mayan World Tree.

20. Why did the Maya sacrifice blood?

21. What three mathematical symbols did the Maya use?

22. What was the Calendar Round?

23. What was the Popul Vuh?

24. How do we know the Toltecs were warlike?

25. Describe the Castillo of Chichen Itza.

PROJECTS

1. Make a map of Mesoamerica, showing major geographical features, such as lakes, mountains, and rivers. Using a color key, indicate the elevation (above or below sea level). Label the major sites you've learned about in this chapter.

2. You learned that the Olmec artists used a purple dye derived from a sea mollusk. Phoenicia (an ancient civilization that flourished in what is now Lebanon) was famous for a similar purple dye. Find out more about how the Phoenicians obtained their purple color.

3. The Olmec craftsmen cut jade with a string and wet sand. Try the process yourself, using an ordinary rock. How long does it take you to make a groove? Report your findings to the class.

4. The Feathered Snake was worshipped by many ancient Americans. Make a chart indicating the places (and dates) that this creature was revered as a god. Then draw your own version of a Feathered Snake.

5. Consult some books about the design of Teotihuacan. Then make a detailed map or model of the city.

6. Build a model of the Pyramid of the Sun using sugar cubes and white glue.

7. Find out more about ancient Egyptian pyramids. Then write an essay comparing them to their Mayan counterparts. Be sure to explain the differences and similarities.

8. The Mixtec lived in mountain villages in southern Mexico They were known as the Cloud People. According to their legends, their ancestors had descended from the skies to the crags of their homeland. They created a rich culture and produced some wonderful art. Their most famous leader was named Eight-Deer Ocelot-Claw. The Mixtec challenged the power of the Zapotecs in the 13th century, AD. Find out more about this interesting people and write a report.

9. Make a timeline of the major events of Mayan history.

10. The Maya believed the underworld consisted of nine levels. Find out about THE INFERNO by Dante, an Italian poet of the early Renaissance. Then write a short essay comparing the Mayan Underworld to that of Dante. (You'll need to find out a bit more about Mayan religious views as well.)

11. Check out the ancient Egyptian and Greek views of the underworld. Then write a short report comparing them to the Mayan concept of the afterlife. (Be sure to include the role of the dog in the Greek underworld.)

12. The Mayan god of the face of the sun spent the day traveling across the heavens and the night in the underworld. The ancient Egyptians had a similar god, named Ra. Find out more about him, and then write a report, comparing the two gods.

13.Let's do some Mayan math. Take the number 25. In our system, 2 stands for 2 tens (20) and 5 stands for 5 ones (or 5). But a Mayan priest would write a bar for the 5 and, just above it, he would write one dot, representing 20. Reading from the top down, this gives 25. To show the number 817, he would write three bars and two dots (17 x 1 = 17), above them one shell (no twenties) and above that two dots (2 x 400 = 800). Reading from top to bottom and adding as you go, you should get 837 (800 + 20 + 17).Now write the following numbers in Mayan mathematical symbols: 57, 389, 462, and 1,357.

14. Spend some time studying the food consumed by the Maya. Make a menu for a Mayan meal. Then have a Mayan feast with your classmates.

15. In about 300 BC a huge circular pyramid 400 feet high was built in Cuicuilco (near Mexico City). Find out more about it and write a report.

3 HAPPENINGS IN SOUTH AMERICA

The first Americans survived because they learned to adapt to the natural environments in which they found themselves. This was not always an easy thing to do. The American continents are vast, and anyone traveling through them will discover a great variety of terrain and climate. But it was in a wide strip of land bordering the west coast of South America (modern Peru and parts of Ecuador, Bolivia, and Chile) that the early immigrants

SOUTH AMERICA

PACIFIC OCEAN

ATLANTIC OCEAN

The shaded region in the map above is the area we will be studying in this chapter. The Amazonian rainforest lies just east of it. In this diverse region of mountains, deserts, and river valleys the first South Americans accomplished some pretty amazing feats!

encountered perhaps the most striking array of contrasting land-scapes and climates — everything from blistering heat to alpine snowfall and tropical rain. In fact, this small part of the world holds a number of geographical world records. Let's take a look at it, moving from west to east.

To begin with, the narrow plain that runs along the Pacific coast for 1,400 miles is the world's driest desert. Rain might not fall here for a century or more! Rising from the flat coastal region are arid hillsides, which are cut in several places by rivers flowing toward the sea. Further east loom the rugged Andes Mountains — the longest mountain range in the world, and one of the highest. The grassy upland valleys of the Andes are surrounded by towering peaks, some of which soar 22,000 feet above sea level. The tallest peaks have snow year round, and many have permanent glaciers. In spring and summer, some of the melting Andean ice drains into Lake Titicaca (Tee tee KAH kah), the world's highest navigable lake. The wooded eastern slopes of the Andes descend into the thick tropical rainforest of the basin of the world's largest and mightiest river, the Amazon. This wet and soggy region receives over 30 feet of rainfall every year.

When the first people arrived in South America, the environment was much as it is today. In this chapter you'll be learning primarily about the people who settled in the desert and mountain regions, because that's where most of the ancient artifacts (and human remains) have been found. The dry heat of the desert and the frigid cold of the mountains preserve organic materials — everything from cloth to human skin — for millennia, while in damper places everything except stone quickly rots and deteriorates. (This is why our knowledge of the Maya depends upon the figures and glyphs they carved on stone. Unfortunately, the ancient peoples of South America had no written language.)

> To be navigable, a body of water must be deep and wide enough for a ship to sail across it. Lake Titicaca easily meets this requirement, being 138 miles long and 70 miles across at its widest point and 940 feet at its deepest place.
>
> The lake lies on the border of modern Peru and Bolivia. It is fed by 25 tributaries flowing from the mountain peaks. The only native fish are killifish and catfish.
>
> Modern steamboats and reed boats (balsas) similar to those of ancient times are used to connect the lakeside settlements.

THE MOUNTAIN DWELLERS

The first nomads arrived in South America over 12,000 years ago and traveled south along the coast. Many of them ventured into the Peruvian Andes and established hunting camps in the upland valleys. There weren't many trees in those high altitudes, but there was certainly plenty of rock, and it became their major building material. The earliest settlers lived in primitive huts of dirt and rocks, but later on the mountain dwellers built sturdier stone houses with clay floors and roofs fashioned from branches gathered from the lower mountain slopes. Each house had several small rooms, with a sunken fire pit in the main one. This is, of course, where the cooking was done. When the sun went down and the air became chilly, the family snuggled together around the warm hearth, talking about the day's activities before going to sleep on their woven grass mats.

By 7000 BC the mountain people had become America's first farmers. (They predated the farmers of Mexico by nearly two thousand years!) They first grew squash, and later learned to cultivate beans, chili peppers, and peanuts. They also experimented with other plants that thrived in the cool, mountain air. Their greatest success was the potato, which they discovered growing wild in the highlands. The potato does well in a cold climate because the edible part is a tuber (the enlarged end of a stem) that grows underground. The potato quickly became a staple of the family diet.

A Llama

(According to some modern food experts, a diet of potatoes and milk will supply all the nutrients the human body needs!)

The mountain valleys were the home of the descendants of the American camel— llamas, alpacas, vicunas, and guanacos. The settlers easily tamed the llamas and alpacas, although the other two species proved difficult to domesticate. They used the soft, lustrous wool of the alpaca for clothing and blankets. The llama's wool is much coarser, so at first this animal was used as a source of meat and leather. Eventually, however, the people discovered that the sure-footed llama could serve them better as a pack animal. It could carry up to 90 pounds of materials over the treacherous mountain trails. (The llama was America's only beast of burden until the Spanish explorers "reintroduced" the horse in the 16th century.) In time, the llama would be a key factor in the development of a vast trading network in the Andes.

Sometimes the herders pierced the ears of their llama and strung colored yarn through the holes.

This gentle, long eye-lashed creature certainly provided a lot for the mountain people — wool, transport of goods, leather, and food (milk as well as meat). Its fat was used in oil lamps. Even its dung was used, both for fuel and for fertilizer. In time, the llama became so essential to life in the mountains that many people actually worshipped its image. (Unfortunately for the llamas, this meant that prize animals were sacrificed to appease the ancient gods!)

THE COASTAL DWELLERS

The nomadic bands who settled along the Peruvian coast found that they could live quite well by fishing. (This region is, in fact, one of the world's richest fishing grounds, due to the warm current — the Humbolt Current.)By 3,000 BC, many villages had sprung up. Fishermen guided their small boats out to sea just a short distance to where billions and billions of tiny anchovies swarmed to feed on the plankton carried by the warm current. They easily scooped up huge quantities of the fish. Most of the anchovies were dried and ground into a fish meal that was rich in protein and easy to preserve.

Other newcomers settled slightly inland along the fertile floodplains of the rivers that wended their way across the desert floor. They fished in the rivers and hunted the small game that came to the riverbanks to drink. Some even trained their dogs to help them hunt the game. (Dogs were the first animals to be tamed by early man. In fact, the dog has been "man's best friend" for over 140,000 years!)

Fairly early, the river dwellers discovered that they could plant squash seeds in the fertile soil of the floodplain. (They

Even in those very early times, there was a certain amount of communication among people living in the various regions of western South America.

Knowledge of farming probably spread down from the mountain valleys to the coastal plain. Many of the lowland plants might have first been planted in the Amazonian jungle, but because of the moisture, there is little evidence of them preserved for archaeologists to study.

probably learned about farming from the mountain dwellers.) The meaty flesh of the squash added variety to their diet of fish and game, and its skin made an excellent waterproof container for liquids. Dried gourds also proved to be ideal floats for the fish-nets. The farmers later learned to grow beans, peppers, avocados, and sweet potatoes. (Corn was not grown in this region until about 2500 BC.) And once they began to grow cotton, they had a useful source of material for weaving fishnets and cloth. (They had no loom, so they twisted the fibers together into cloth using a method similar to crocheting.)

The inhabitants of each farming village (known as an *ayllu*) shared the ownership of the surrounding land. Every family was responsible for providing a certain amount of labor in the fields, and at harvest time the crops were distributed equally. As the population grew, there was a greater demand for food. Seeking ways to expand the size of their yield, the farmers stumbled upon the basic principles of irrigation — channeling water from a river into parts of a nearby field. (Remember what a breakthrough this was for the Mesoamerican farmers?) Irrigation enabled the river dwellers to harvest much larger quantities of crops. Around 1750 BC, villagers in the Rimac River Valley built a canal that was four miles long. They dug the main channel as well as the smaller ones that branched off of it using only wooden digging sticks. This project was quite an accomplishment for those ancient times, and it quadrupled the amount of farmland!

Now that there was ample food, some of the settlers could specialize in tasks like making pottery or weaving cloth. This, of course, marked the beginning of civilization. (Remember how the same thing happened in Mesoamerica?) Gradually, village society was divided into separate classes — (1) the farmers, hunters and fishermen, (2) the craftsmen, and (3) the ruling chiefs (who inher-ited their power) and priests. As was the case further north, the local ruler was often also the chief priest.

We know a great deal about the people of the coastal region because of the way they buried their dead. The bodies were wrapped in reeds and cotton leaves and placed in shallow graves, often with practical objects like pots and tools for use in the afterlife. Because of the dryness of the region (tissue-destroy-ing bacteria cannot survive without moisture), these "natural" mummies have been preserved for thousands of years. So far, archaeologists have uncovered over 2,000 of them, and there are probably many more still buried in the ground. Most of the mummies that have been unearthed are less than 5,000 years old (dating from about 3000 BC), but some date back 8,000 years (making them much, much older than the more famous mummies of Egypt.) By examining these ancient remains, archaeologists have discovered that the early settlers had good teeth, probably because they ate few carbohydrates. However, many people apparently died of pneumonia. No one is certain why.

When someone really important died, he (or she) was often buried in a tomb — the more important the person was, the larger the tomb. As early as 3000 BC, the people living in Aspero, Peru built an impressive tomb in the form of a huge flat-topped pyramid. It was the world's first monumental pyramid. To construct it, workers filled thousands of bags woven from grasses with rubble (rocks and pebbles) and used them as building blocks. Then they faced the giant structure with stone and built a temple on top. Human remains have been recovered from the pyramid, as well as the buried offerings of dogs and guinea pigs.

> The pyramid tomb in Peru was built nearly 2,000 years before the Olmecs built theirs.
> The "Age of Pyramids" in ancient Egypt also came later — roughly between 2700 and 2200 BC.

Smaller pyramid tombs have also been found, many with multiple graves. Apparently, the graves were dug into the flat summit of the pyramid tomb. But after many years, the "cemetery" would be full. What then? The villagers simply tore down the temple and covered the top of the mound with fresh layers of rubble and earth. Then they built a new temple. Now they had plenty of room to dig a new grave. A cross-section of one of these pyramids is like a giant layer cake. Digging from top to bottom, archaeologists have unearthed a series of time capsules conveniently arranged in chronological order, dating from the most recent to the oldest.

THE JUNGLE DWELLERS

The bands of migrating tribesmen who stumbled into the rainforest must have been dazzled by the abundance of plant and animal life they found there. Even today, there is a wider variety of species in a single acre of the rainforest than anywhere else on the planet. Many people settled there. In time, they learned to hunt animals with blowguns — hollowed bamboo sticks through which thcy blcw dcadly poisonous arrows. The poison was made from curare, a plant substance, which instantly paralyzed the prey. (The lungs couldn't function and the animal died of suffocation.) The jungle dwellers made fish hooks out of bone and wove fishing nets from plant fibers. They even figured out how to stun fish by sprinkling plant products similar to curare upon the water.

Today curare is often used (in small doses!) with anesthesia in surgery to cause muscles to relax.

Although they were mostly hunters and gatherers, the jungle dwellers did grow a few crops. One that is still grown in Brazil is the tropical plant called cassava (also known as manioc). It has a twisted stem and grows to the height of about three feet. It has tuberous roots (like the potato), which have been a staple of the jungle dwellers for thousands of years. The cassava root can be dangerous, however. It contains a poison, prussic acid, which is the source of cyanide! The natives learned to remove the poison by peeling, grating, washing, squeezing, and toasting the roots and then grinding the remains into flour. They used the flour to make bread or a sort of pudding. (You might have had some pudding made from the cassava. It's called tapioca.)

Life could be violent in the jungle. Some of the tribesmen were cannibals (throwing the flesh of their victims into a pot of stew), while others cut off the heads of their slain enemies, shrunk them, and wore them as trophies! As you will see, this became a fairly popular fad in ancient South America.

As more and more people settled in the regions you've been reading about — the coastal desert, the floodplain and foothills, the highlands, and, to a lesser degree, the jungle — trade became more common.

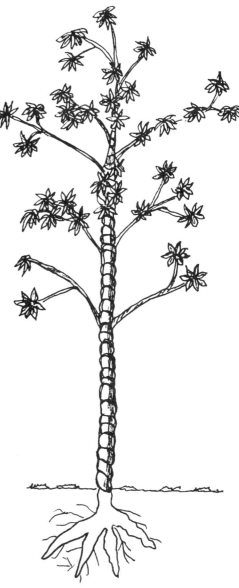

A Cassava Tree

We know, for example, that the highland people often traded with natives living along the Pacific coast, because seashells have been found in Andean garbage dumps, while obsidian, which occurs only in the mountains, has turned up among the ruins and graves of lowland settlements.

CHAVIN DE HUANTAR — CIVILIZATION BEGINS

High on the eastern slopes of the Andes Mountains, overlooking a tributary of the mighty Amazon River, there once stood a magnificent complex of stone temples. This was Chavin de Huantar (Chav VEEN day WAHN tar). Farmers and herders had lived in this scenic valley for centuries, but around 800 BC the region became an important center of trade and religious pilgrimages. And this was only the beginning! The influence of the local culture (known as Chavin culture) grew and grew until, four centuries later when it reached its peak, Chavin de Huantar had become the heart of South America's earliest civilization, influencing the lives of thousands of people.

When the population of the valley first began to expand, the farmers worried about being able to grow enough crops. The problem was not a lack of water, as it was in the coastal region, but the limited amount of flat, arable land. (There's not much of that in the mountains!) The ingenious farmers found the solution (and gained countless acres of new farmland) by cutting terraces into the mountainsides. These rose like a series steps from the valley floor. Each terrace, or step, was lined with stone to prevent the dirt from washing away, and stone gutters carried away the excess water. Now the farmers could grow larger quantities of vegetables. (Similar techniques are still used in the Andes today.)

Little by little, the classes of Chavin society became more distinct. As you'd expect, the lines were drawn between the rulers and priests, the artisans, and the farmers.

Chavin weavers were the first in South America to use a loom. Theirs was a small and simple device known as a back loom. Here's how it worked. The warp (the lengthwise thread of wool) was looped and stretched between two poles. One pole, parallel to the ground, was attached to a tree sapling, and the other was tied to a strap, which encircled the waist of the weaver. The weaver controlled the tension (tightness) of the warp threads by leaning back and forth. She wove the crosswise threads

Weaving on a Back Loom

through the vertical ones using a shuttle — a piece of bone or wood with a hole at one end to which the thread was attached. With every new row, she would lean back to tighten the threads that she had woven.

The beautiful woolen cloth produced on such a loom became a source of prestige and wealth throughout the Andes. Llama wool was used for everyday items, like winter cloaks and blankets. The softer wool of the alpaca, vicuna, and guanaco were reserved for luxury fabrics. (The wool was plucked off the backs of these animals when they were molting.) Strands of the raw wool were twisted around a wooden spindle and slowly spun into a long, single thread. The wool was colored with vegetable and animal dyes.

Artists often painted figures of jungle animals on the finished cloth. The most common figure was a snarling jaguar with clenched teeth and overlapping fangs — the most fearsome of the Chavin gods. He appears again and again, not only on the cloth but also on pottery and on the stone walls of temples and obelisks (free-standing stone pillars). This, of course, was the same creature worshipped by so many peoples of Mesoamerica. In earlier times, the jaguar ruled as supreme king of beasts throughout much of Central and South America. Even today, the jaguar is probably the most ferocious beast prowling the Amazonian rainforest. The ancient people of Chavin certainly feared him, even though they lived high above the jungle and only heard tales about him. But they also marveled at his grace, power, and strength. The jaguar was usually associated with rain.

> Even today, the Quechua tribes-men of the Peruvian Andes believe that a catlike god, *Coa*, roams the highlands and brings hail and light-ning, often destroying their crops.

(Why? Perhaps because the people believed that the jaguar was so powerful it could do anything, like make it rain! Or maybe they made this association because the jaguar prowled about the rain-forest.)

Another creature sacred to the Chavin people was the snake. As you've learned, many primitive cultures associated it with regeneration, and since it slithered along the ground, often hiding beneath the undergrowth, it was also connected with the unseen underworld. The cayman, that fierce-looking crocodillian, was apparently the Chavin god of rivers. There's no mystery about this association!

Now that you know something about Chavin deities, let's take a close look at the temple complex at Chavin de Huantar. The main temple was actually a 50-foot-tall truncated pyramid. At one time there was probably an adobe structure with a thatched roof on its sum-mit, but most of the temple rooms were within the pyramid itself. Two staircases, lined with carvings of jaguars and eerie-looking half human figures, led to the flat top. They faced east toward the mountains — the direction of the rising sun. From each side of the pyramid extended a long earthen mound. The three

> Spanish explorers called the main temple pyramid of Chavin de Huantar the *Castillo*, their word for "castle." They clearly had no idea of the purpose of the giant structure!

giant structures (the pyramid and the two mounds) formed a U and towered above a sunken central plaza. Most of the religious ceremonies took place in the plaza. The entire complex covered 12 acres. (That's about 20 football fields!)

The priests lived on wide terraces surrounding the main temple. These men were all-powerful, not only in matters of reli-gion but in every other aspect of Chavin society. When they performed religious rituals, they often chewed upon the buds of the mescal cactus or the leaves of the coca tree (the source of cocaine) in order to enter a hallucinogenic trance. (The purpose of this was to enable them to see visions, to "go beyond" the everyday world around them.) Try to envision the performing priests, dancing about in woven kilts and animal skins, burdened by large golden headdresses adorned with exotic bird feathers and gleaming with golden jewelry — earrings, nose ornaments, and lip plugs. (Sometimes the earrings were so heavy that they grossly distorted the earlobes from which they hung.)

This ugly, snarling fanged creature was carved on one of the outer walls of the main temple.

The main temple pyramid actually consisted of several platforms of descending size, built one upon another. These were constructed at several different times. Each platform was made of rubble and faced with alternating rows of large and small stone (basalt) blocks set in clay mortar. The Chavin leaders had to be skillful managers to direct the many thousands of laborers required to build such a massive complex. Many similar pyramids were built throughout the surrounding region. One structure required 100,000 tons of quarried basalt to cover it.

The pyramid was honeycombed with narrow, windowless galleries and passages, many connected by stairways. No one is sure of their purpose. Even more puzzling are the subterranean channels that carried river water through and under the huge structure. The sounds of the rushing currents of water must have produced a dramatic effect! But why were the channels constructed in the first place? Many scholars believe that the temple complex was devoted to the worship of water, that life-giving fluid so crucial to life.

Water worship was common in ancient America. High in the Colombian Andes, a 150 foot square rock was carved as a monument, right in the bed of a torrent of cascading water. This was a sacred site in which to worship the water that tumbled down the mountain slopes to the sea.

In one section of the temple, at the intersection of two galleries, stood a 13-foot-high free-standing stone sculpture of a snarling creature, half jaguar, half human, with snakes forming its eyebrows and hair. Its right clawed arm was raised in defiance. The entire statue was bathed in sunlight coming from openings cut into the stone above it. Imagine walking along a dark, window-less gallery, hearing the sounds of the water and then suddenly encountering this creature! If the statue was intended to make the worshipper feel humble and small before the awesome power of the gods, it certainly achieved the desired effect! This statue, known as the Smiling God (although Snarling God would be more accurate!), is the oldest ceremonial object in the Americas that is still in its original setting. Some archaeologists believe that the statue might have played a role in an oracle. (An oracle was a shrine where predictions were made about the future. There were many oracles in the ancient world, the most famous being the Oracle of Delphi in Greece.) Prophesies might have been shouted down by priests in the chambers above to worshippers kneeling before the statue. (A groove ran from the statue's hand to its nose and might have pointed to the rooms above.)

Many examples of fearsome-looking creatures have been found among the ruins of other Chavin temples throughout Peru. Some depict ferocious animals — writhing snakes, snarling caymans, and fierce birds of prey, like eagles and hawks. Others are scary-looking supernatural figures — part human, part jungle beast. Carving these creatures was not easy, since the stoneworkers had no metal chisels. Like the Mesoamericans, they depended upon their

> Why were the figures often depicted as half-human, half-beast? Perhaps the Chavin priests wore animal masks when they performed religious rites, as well as the skins. The carvings might represent the priests themselves, who served as communicators between the people and the spirits. (Many scholars use this reasoning to explain the animal-headed human-bodied gods of the ancient Egyptians.)

> At the center of a typical Chavin temple was a fire pit. Here offerings, such as seashells, animals, and plants were made to the gods. When chili peppers were thrown into the fire they produced an acrid smoke that brought tears to the eyes of the worshippers. This shedding of tears probably symbolized the falling of rain and was an appeal to the rain gods.

stone tools and the corrosive effect of sand and water to create their figures and designs.

As you'd expect, much of Chavin religion had to do with pacifying the fearsome gods who seemed to control the forces of nature. Sacrifices were common. Litter found at some ceremonial sites includes the remains of food as well as the bones of domestic animals, such as the guinea pig and the llama. Archaeologists have also discovered the skulls of human beings.

Fierce jungle creatures were the subjects of many other forms of art. The snarling feline mouths and crossed fangs appeared again and again on small statuettes, in decorations of ceramic jugs, and in the intricate designs of gold and silver jewelry. (There were numerous gold and silver mines in the Andes. The long-suffering miners formed the lowest class of Chavin society.)

> Chavin craftsmen experimented with metal-working techniques, such as soldering, welding, and alloying (mixing) gold and silver. However, like other prehistoric peoples of America, they never learned to melt down metals to mold them into tools and other objects. They simply heated the raw ore (using blowpipes to increase the heat of their charcoal fires) and then pounded it into the shapes they wanted.

The beliefs and lifestyle of the Chavin people spread far and wide, thanks to their extensive trading network. So when Chavin de Huantar fell into decline about 200 BC (for reasons unknown), its rich culture continued to thrive, in one form or another, for a long, long time. Among those peoples most influenced by the Chavin culture were three societies that flourished along the coast — the Paracas, Nazca, and Moche. The Paracas, using the back loom, improved upon Chavin weaving techniques and created some of the ancient world's most beautiful cloth. The Nazca copied the ceramics of Chavin potters and then developed their own distinctive style of clay vessel. The Moche were master metalsmiths, and they, too, owed much to Chavin craftsmen. Let's take a closer look at each of these cultures. See how many connections you can make between them and the Chavin people.

THE PARACAS — MASTER EMBROIDERERS

The Paracas (Pa RAH kas) people lived on the Paracas peninsula (this explains their name!) that juts along Peru's southern coast. Most of what we know about the Paracas comes from the deep, bottle-shaped tombs that they built between 700 and 200 BC. Each tomb was lined with adobe bricks and accommodated at least 40 bodies. Each of the bodies was carefully wrapped in many layers of cloth (as many as 50 layers!) to form a thick bundle. Cotton garments — shirts, mantles, loincloths, and burbans — were tucked between the layers. The body bundles were placed in the tomb in large woven baskets.

It's the beautiful woolen cloth that most interests archaeologists. After all these centuries, the colors have remained rich and vivid because of the dry desert air. (The bodies, too, have been preserved as natural mummies, complete with hair and fingernails.) The weavers could only produce cloth about three feet wide on their back looms, so these were sewn together to form larger pieces of material. Rather than paint designs on the cloth as the Chavin artists had done, the Paracas embroidered their designs on their cloth. They covered each piece with hundreds of small figures — warriors, dancers, jungle creatures (particularly snakes and cats), and composite beasts like bird-people. Using tiny overlapping stitches, they created extremely fine details. Often as many as 22 different colors were used in a single figure.

A Figure Woven on a Paracas Cloth

The pictures on the cloth give us a good idea of what the Paracas people looked like. And the large number of armed warriors depicted suggests that they were more warlike than the Chavin. (No fortifications or stashes of weapons have ever been detected at Chavin sites, nor is there any warlike motif in their art.) Apparently, the Paracas collected the heads of their fallen enemies as trophies, since the body of one of their gods appears covered with grim-looking shrunken heads! This strange deity also had dangling limbs and huge staring eyes,

which earned him the nickname of *Oculate Being* ("Eye Guy")
among modern scholars. Compared to the grizzly Eye Guy, the
jungle cats embroidered into the cloth seem fairly tame!

THE NAZCA — LINE MAKERS

The Nazca lived in two adjoining river valleys along the
coast of southern Peru, beginning around 200 BC. Their capital
city contained several terraced pyramids. The largest, 65 feet
high, towered above a central plaza and several stone tombs.

The Nazca fished, hunted, and grew fruits and vegetables
in the parched desert land, which they irrigated via a network of
long canals. Nazca potters produced some of the finest ceramics
in ancient America. Many of their brightly painted pots were decorated with figures of gods, people, animals, birds, and plants
that resemble those embroidered on the Paracas cloth. (This is
not surprising, since the Paracas and Nazca traded with one
another.) Other pots were decorated with bold geometric designs.

Like the Paracas, the Nazca warriors took heads as battle
trophies and worshipped "Eye Guy." They battled their enemies
with war clubs, bashing skulls right and left! Maybe this is why
they developed a medical technique to treat head wounds.
Trepanning is a method of cutting open a living person's skull to
relieve pain and pressure from swelling caused by wounds or disease. A Nazca priest (priests were regarded as healers) removed a
piece of skull by cutting a hole with an obsidian knife. Or he
might simply scrape away the bare bone after removing part of
the skin. Sounds terrible, doesn't it? But, surprisingly, many Nazca
patients recovered from successful skull surgery. How do we
know? Because skulls have been found that provide evidence of
wounds that have healed.

The Nazca also produced beautifully decorated cloth.
(Have you noticed the importance of woven cloth in ancient
Peru? Even today, the descendants of the people we are studying
are famous for their woolen cloth.) The Nazca wove their designs
rather than paint or embroider them. Many priceless pieces of
their cloth have been discovered buried with their dead.
(Archaeologists believe that the Nazca wove most of their cloth
specifically to be buried.)

At the time of burial, a body was placed in a squatting
position, knees against the chest, and bound with many yards of

the cloth. Like the Paracas, the Nazca often included objects, such as gold ornaments, feather fans, and even bits of food in the cloth bundle. The bodies were buried in circular pits in the desert floor, where they have remained well preserved until modern times.

The most interesting legacy of the Nazca is the series of ground drawings (known as the "Nazca lines") that they carved onto the sun-burnished surface of the desert. (These are technically called *geoglyphs*, or "earth carvings.") Over 300 giant-sized figures of animals and elaborate networks of straight lines and geometric shapes cover an area of almost 200 square miles. Many generations of Nazca created the figures by scraping away the dark, weathered surface stones and gravel to expose the lighter-colored earth beneath. They highlighted the edges of the figures by lining them with piles of the darker gravel.

The lines vary from 600 yards to more than eight miles in length and form spirals and zigzags, triangles and trapezoids. There are even webs of arrow-straight lines that cross one another or come together at a central point. Among the animal figures are birds (18 kinds!), a spider, a killer whale, and a monkey with a long spiraling tail. The beak of a hummingbird consists of two parallel lines, each 120 feet long! Since there is no rain in this desert region to disturb the ground, most of the lines remain just as they were made over 1,000 years ago!

What is truly amazing is that the figures can only be seen in full from aloft. We can appreciate them from an airplane window, but how could those ancient artists design such symmetrical and precise figures without being able to "stand back" and view the entire piece? And why did they do it? The lines have puzzled archaeologists for a long time. Some have suggested that, since they can only be appreciated from the heavens, they were intended for the enjoyment, or appeasement, of the gods. Others believe that they represent pattern of the sun, moon, and stars, and thus were used as a kind of calendar. (Some lines align with the setting sun at certain times of the year, such as the winter solstice.) Or perhaps they marked ritual pathways and connect sacred sites. We'll probably never know for sure how and why the lines were made.

Around 700 AD, the Nazca fell under the influence of people from the highlands to the east, and their culture began to fade. It soon disappeared, along with the answers to our questions.

Nazca lines are in danger! Maria Reiche, a valiant woman who defended them for 50 years, died in 1998 at the age of 95. Maria believed the designs represented a giant calendar based upon the movements of constellations. She had fought off all kinds of threats to the lines, including plans to hold a motorcycle race across them and to irrigate the region for farming.

On July 23, 1998, tourists from California, after dumping fruit peels and egg shells from their van, drove across the lines. Their tire tracks scarred the fragile, ancient designs and will remain there for centuries. And there are other dangers! At night looters dig there in search of Indian graves, miners look for gold, and city trucks dump their garbage! The busy Pan American Highway, built in the early 1940's, slices hundreds of lines and cuts a drawing of a giant lizard in two.

The Peruvian government budgets $10,000 annually to protect the site, but this only pays for two guards on motorcycles to patrol the 200 square miles of desert. At night, they go home, and there's no one at all to protect what have been called the world's largest hieroglyphs. Centuries of neglect have destroyed about a fifth of the original etchings. What does the future hold for them?

THE MOCHE — EMPIRE BUILDERS

The warlike Moche (MO chee) controlled much of northern Peru between 200 and 700 AD, including more than 150 miles along the coast. They began as simple farmers, but as their numbers grew they gradually became a complex society controlled by lords who ruled the river valleys. Theirs is the earliest empire we know about in South America. They are named after the Moche River near the coast, where their main religious and government center was located.

The Moche mastered the techniques of irrigation and constructed a vast network of canals and aqueducts to bring water to over a hundred thousand acres of arid land. This enabled them to produce seven times more crops than modern farmers harvest in that area today. One canal carried water 75 miles from its source to the fields.

Their main crop was corn (an import from the north), which was usually roasted over a fire and eaten on the cob. Sometimes the women pressed oil from the kernels or even fermented them to make beer. The farmers also grew beans, peppers, peanuts, squash, avocado, papaya, pineapple, and cotton. They gathered guano (bird droppings) from offshore islands and used it as fertilizer.

The Moche raised llamas, ducks, and guinea pigs for food. Fishermen built canoe-like rafts from bundles of reeds lashed together and netted huge amounts of anchovy, crab, and shrimp. The wealthy lords, using teams of dogs, hunted the deer that roamed the wooded hills. Members of the lower classes were forbidden to hunt deer — the punishment was death! (Did you know that the same thing was true in medieval Europe?)

The Moche produced enough food to support about 100,000 people. Today only 7,000 people can survive in that arid region. How can this be? Although modern technology could easily work miracles in that region, the present inhabitants of coastal Peru are fairly poor. They produce just enough to get along.

Moche metalsmiths produced some of the finest gold, silver, and copper ornamental objects in America. They smelted the ores in clay ovens and fashioned them into luxury items like copper masks, gold earspools (huge, rounded earrings), bracelets, and nose rings, helmets and headdresses, gorgettes (a large pendant worn just below the throat), and small statues. Recently, a number of rich tombs have been discovered — including those of a warrior priest and a priestess. Among the artifacts buried were exquisite gold and turquoise earspools, each depicting warriors that are, in turn, wearing exquisite earspools!

Moche sculptors invented a lost-wax method of casting hollow metal figures, similar to the method used in ancient civilizations of the Mediterranean Sea. Here's how an artist went about the task. First the sculptor created a heat resistant model of clay mixed with carbon, coated it with a thin layer of wax, and sculpted details into the wax layer's surface. Then he applied a layer of heat-proof clay over the wax, making two carefully positioned holes through the clay before it hardened. When the molten metal was poured into one of the holes in this outer mold, it melted the wax and pushed it out the other hole. After the metal hardened, the clay molds were broken to remove the newly cast figure.

Moche potters learned to make ceramic half-molds cast from a solid model of a particular figure so that they could actually mass produce identical pots. To make a pot the two half-molds were lined with layers of wet clay. Once the clay began to harden, the molds were removed and the two clay pieces were joined. Then, after the stirrup-shaped spout and other decorations were added, the pot was painted and then fired. The pots were made in the shape of human beings, deities, animals, and even buildings. The human portraits, in particular, were extremely realistic. Some of the pots were painted with scenes from every-day life — there are hunters stalking their prey, warriors battling their enemies, musicians, dancers, and even priests chewing cocoa leaves beneath a starry sky. The potters could even make pitchers that whistled! (Air was sucked in through tiny vents as the liquid was poured out.)

This is a whistling pitcher. The air was sucked in through a vent just above the face. The handle is known as a "stirrup handle" because of its shape. This type of handle was very typical in Moche pottery.

Fortunately for us, many of these pots were also buried in graves and have survived intact. The body of one wealthy lord was surrounded with 75 of them! As with the cloth of the other cultures we've been learning about, the figures on the Moche ceramics provide vivid pictures of how the people lived. They are the closest thing we have to a written history.

A major Moche god appears often on the pots. He was no beauty — he had a human face and body, but the fangs of a jaguar. Sometimes he appears with dragon-like spines. Apparently, this fearsome deity demanded human blood. One pot depicts the headless body of a victim lying at his feet. He apparently did the deed himself, since he holds a sacrificial knife (*tumi*) in one hand. (You'll see him on the next page.) Moche warriors tried to capture their enemies rather than kill them so that they could later be sacrificed. (There was even a hierarchy in the treatment of sacrificial victims. Ordinary people walked to the altar to have their throats slit, but captured noblemen were carried there in litters!)

As the population grew, the Moche extended their territory into neighboring valleys until they controlled about 400 miles along the coast, which extended inland to the mountains. Like the Nazca, they had a trade network that extended far beyond their own borders. For example, they imported stones such as turquoise from Chile (hundreds of miles to the south) and rare seashells came Ecuador (hundreds of miles to the north). Examples of their pottery have been found all along the coast and throughout the Andean highlands. Many of the roads they built would become part of the Inca highway system 900 years later.

The Moche constructed hundreds of truncated temple pyramids. Their most impressive structures were the pyramids in their capital city, known as the Pyramid of the Sun and the Pyramid of the Moon. (These names were given them by Spanish explorers centuries later— actually, the pyramids had nothing to do with the sun or the moon. The same thing happened in Teotihuacan, didn't it?) Both structures consisted of ascending tiers of platforms, similar to the temple pyramid in Chavin de Huantar.

This is a Moche ceramic pot known as "Decapitator." It depicts a blood-thirsty god holding a sacrificial knife in one hand and the head of his victim in the other!

The Pyramid of the Sun was the largest pyramid in South America. (It was not quite as large as Teotihuacan's Pyramid of the Sun, which held the record.) Made of 50 million sun-baked adobe bricks, it was 522 feet wide, 1,150 feet long, and rose to a height of nearly 150 feet. It covered 12.5 acres in the Moche River Valley. The Pyramid of the Moon was considerably smaller. Paintings on several Moche pots depict prisoners from battle being sacrificed to fanged beings seated on top of the two pyramids. Similar scenes were painted on the walls of temples and government buildings. Did this symbolize a ritual sacrifice, or did the Moche rulers actually drink the blood of their enemies? Once again, we can only guess.

The Moche civilization came to a sudden end. Scientists believe it was destroyed by severe earthquakes followed by torrential rains. By 800 AD, it had disappeared.

Now you know quite a lot about the first South Americans. You've learned about the first Andean civilization (Chavin de Huantar), and the three cultures that were so strongly influenced by it (the Paracas, Nazca, and Moche). Some of these people were mountain dwellers, while others lived in desert regions. Nonetheless, they had many things in common. The weaving and design of cloth is a good example, as is their resourcefulness as

Major Sites of Ancient South America

farmers. They made some beautiful metal jewelry, and yet they never thought about making metal tools. What similarities do you see among their religious views? Can you make any other connections? What do you consider their greatest legacy?

Before leaving this part of the Americas, let's take a peek at two other cultures that evolved somewhat later in Peru — the Tiahuanacans and the Chimu. Look for ways in which they might have been influenced by the earlier inhabitants of that region.

TIAHUANACO

High in the Andes just 12 miles from the eastern shores of Lake Titicaca stood the city of Tiahuanaco (tee ah wah NAH koh). (This was a lofty site, lying at over 12,500 feet above sea level.) The city flourished between 500 and 1000 AD

People had been living near Lake Titicaca for thousands of years, even though it is a bleak treeless plateau. Why? Because this is the largest area of flat farming land in the Andes. Hardy cold-resistant plants like the potato, oca (something like a sweet potato), and quinoa (a rice-like grain) were probably first grown here. Miles of grasslands also provided good grazing for llama and alpaca herds. The local residents became South America's most important breeders of these animals. The lake itself was teeming with fish and waterfowl. Boats were constructed from bundles of reeds (called *totora*) that were tightly packed together to make them waterproof. The totora, which grew abundantly along the banks of the lake, had many other uses. The Tiahuanacans boiled and roasted the bottom stems and then ground them to make flour. They also wove fibers of the reed to make mats and baskets.

The lake dwellers were a very industrious people. As their numbers grew, they reclaimed land from the shores of the lake to extend their farmland. They sent llama caravans down the slopes of the Andes to trade with villages all along the coast to the west

Coca, a plant that is the source of cocaine, was grown in the lower elevations of ancient Peru. You've already learned that it was used for religious rituals, but ordinary travelers to the highlands also nibbled on its long leaves. Sometimes, they mixed the coca leaves with lime produced by burning seashells. This produced a mixture that countered the fatigue humans often experience in thin, high-altitude air.

Interestingly enough, coca leaves are quite nutritious, being rich in Vitamin C and calcium!

and in the rainforest to the east. They even established distant colonies to enrich their trading monopoly.

By 800 AD, Tiahuanaco was a large city of about 40,000 people. It contained a cluster of dazzling temples, courtyards, terraces, and palaces built of enormous cut and polished stones fitted together without mortar. (Some of the stones weighed more than 100 tons and had been dragged from quarries over three miles away.) The stones were so tightly fitted together that a blade of grass could not slip between them.

At the center was a raised temple enclosure. It was entered through a massive gateway known as the Gate of the Sun, which rose about ten feet and was cut from a single block of volcanic stone (andesite). The stone weighed almost 20 tons! At the top of the gate was a carved figure wearing a headdress resembling the rays of the sun and carrying a staff in each hand. Tracks of tears ran down his cheeks. (Given what you've learned so far, what do you think the tears represented?) Condor and puma heads were carved on his body and from his belt hung a row of human faces, perhaps trophy heads from sacrificial victims. Visitors passing beneath the figure must have trembled in fear. He is surrounded by many winged attendants. Because of its placement, some archaeologists believe the Gate of the Sun might have had a use connected with the marking of

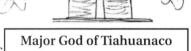

Major God of Tiahuanaco

time. Symbols carved on the stone might represent a calendar. If they do, this would be the world's oldest calendar.

Within the enclosure were many temples. The largest temple platform was 50 feet high and measured 656 square feet at the base. It was decorated with fierce-looking stone human heads.

The Tiahuanacans sacrificed human victims to their gods. Severed skulls, polished so that they look almost like ivory, have been discovered buried in their temples. The skulls were apparently used as cups from which the priests drank an alcoholic beverage!

Although Tiahuanaco seems to have been blessed with many natural resources, the city was eventually abandoned. So far, no one is certain what caused the people to live their highland home.

THE CHIMU

Here's one last group of early South Americans to learn about — the Chimu. They're quite unusual, well worth a moment of study. Around 800 AD, the Chimu began to create an empire that stretched 600 miles along the Peruvian coast. Their capital city, Chan Chan, was the home of a very powerful aristocracy, who made up about a tenth of the Chimu population and ruled the empire.

Chan Chan consisted of 11 separate compounds with interesting trellis-like adobe walls. Each compound was like a small palace, housing a nobleman and his family and servants. Within the walls of each compound was a private temple and pyramid tomb. The Chimu elite viewed themselves as semi-deities, and they had an obsession about their belongings. Thieves were executed, and anyone who defiled a holy shrine was buried alive! When a Chimu nobleman died, he was buried in his pyramid tomb and his property, filled with his luxurious belongings, was permanently sealed off. So little by little, much of the city became a cemetery!

But the rulers were not the only inhabitants of the city. Large numbers of artisans lived in small, windowless apartments near the compounds. They produced excellent works of art, particularly fine ceramics, jewelry, and cloth. Their presence made Chan Chan the largest, most populous city of pre-Columbian South America.

But, as should be clear by now, no culture lasts forever. In the late 15th century, Chan Chan was plundered and destroyed by a new, upcoming force — the legendary Inca. These intruders managed to outshine nearly everyone who lived before them in South America. You'll learn all about these fascinating people in Book II.

The Huari, who lived 700 miles to the north, were major rivals of the Tiahuanacans. Their main city covered over a thousand acres and housed 70,000 people, almost double the population of Tiahuanaco. Huari artisans produced beautiful woolen tapestries, gold and copper jewelry, stone figures, and pottery.

In about 600 AD, the Huari embarked on a series of military conquests — taking over the lands of the Nazca, the Moche, and many others, until they controlled Peru from the Andean peaks to the coast deserts. In the process, they created what was probably the first centralized military empire in South America. It lasted about two more centuries. But around 1200, it, too, faded into obscurity.

REVIEW QUESTIONS

1. Describe the geographical "world records" of the region in and around Peru.
2. What crops did the mountain dwellers grow?
3. What animals were native to the mountain regions?
4. How did the coastal farmers expand their crop production?
5. Why have the bodies of the ancient coastal dwellers survived for so long?
6. How did the jungle dwellers get their food?
7. What was South America's earliest civilization?
8. How did the back loom work?
9. Describe the temple complex at Chavin de Huantar.
10. Describe "Smiling God."
11. How did Paracas cloth differ from that of Chavin?
12. How did Nazca cloth differ from that made by the Paracas?
13. How were the Nazca Lines made?
14. What presently threatens the Nazca Lines?
15. How did the Moche craftsmen make metal figures?
16. What was the largest pyramid in South America?
17. Where was the potato first grown?
18. Describe the Gate of the Sun.
19. How did ChanChan evolve into a giant cemetery?
20. What culture replaced that of the Chimu?

PROJECTS

1. Sixty percent of the varieties of crops that now support the world's population were originally grown by Native Americans. This includes maize, potatoes, manioc (cassava), beans, squash, pumpkins, sweet potatoes, vanilla, tomatoes, chili peppers, pineapples, avocados, gourds, and sunflowers. Using pictures cut from magazines and your own drawings, make a collage of "Native American Plant Foods."

2. Make a detailed geographical map of South America, indicating major landforms and natural features. Be sure to include a key showing elevation.

3. Find out more about the wooly beasts of the Andes — the llama, alpaca, vicuna, and guanaco. Then write a report. Be sure to include illustrations.

4. Learn more about the Peruvian mummies. Then check out how the ancient Egyptians prepared mummies for burial in stone tombs. Write a report comparing these two types of mummy — natural and artificial.

5. Find out what kinds of people currently inhabit the Amazonian rainforest. Make a chart showing how their lives are similar to those of people living there thousands of years ago. Then indicate any differences you discover.

6. Make a clay or papier mache model of the temple complex at Chavin de Huantar.

7. Check the books in your classroom and the library for illustrations of the cloth woven by the early inhabitants of Peru. Then prepare a short presentation in which you show them to your classmates. Begin with general information about weaving and decorating techniques. Explain which features are unique in each type of cloth.

8. Find some illustrations of Chavin priests and read the description on page 71. Then draw a picture of one of these men leading a religious ritual.

9. Find a photograph of "Smiling God" and share it with your classmates.

10. Using the Internet, find out more about the Nazca Lines. What is being done to save them? What needs to be done? How can you help? Present your findings to the class.

12. Make a timeline of the major culture groups and civilizations of South America up to the time of the Inca.

4 THE AMERICAN SOUTHWEST

The American Southwest is a scenic — but arid — region of mountains, mesas, ravines, canyons, and river valleys. It extends from the border of Mexico through Arizona, New Mexico, and across the southern parts of Utah and Colorado. Today, many towns and cities are thriving here, despite the desert heat, thanks to the modern convenience of air conditioning.

At the end of the Ice Age, the natural environment of the Southwest was very different. Because the climate was so much cooler and wetter, there were many rivers and lakes filled with fish, lush meadows of green grass, and scattered woodlands of fir, pine and broad-leafed trees. Like the Great Plains of those early times, this pleasant region attracted large grazing animals like the mammoth and mastodon. Herds of antelope flocked to the gently rolling grasslands, while deer, elk, and bighorn sheep foraged in the forested hills and mountains.

> A mesa is a high, flat landform. It looks something like a mountain that has been sliced off halfway up with a giant knife. The word "mesa" means table in Spanish, and, from a distance, a mesa certainly *does* look like a huge table of rock. The French call this type of landform a plateau, and this term is also commonly used in English.

The hunters who arrived in the Southwest thousands of years ago certainly had no difficulty finding enough to eat, and they readily took advantage of the bounties of nature. In the warmer seasons, they lived in the small huts they made by piling brush over a crude framework of branches. With the coming of winter, they moved into the caves that had been gouged out of the sides of the steep canyons by centuries of wind and rain. The most inviting caves faced south, catching the warmest sun for a few hours each day during the cold winters.

You've already learned how some of the hunters learned to make rather good stone spear points. (Remember the Clovis and Folsum cultures of New Mexico?) No one is certain whether these points were first made in the Southwest or the Great Plains, but knowledge of how to make them had spread far and wide by 8000 BC.

THE WARMING

As the temperature of the planet rose and the glaciers receded, the Southwest changed dramatically and began to look the way it does today. No longer did northerly breezes carry down moisture from the melting edges of the sheets of ice, and mountains to the west and east, some with peaks above 14,000 feet, prevented rain clouds from the Pacific Ocean and the Gulf of Mexico from reaching the region. So the lakes dried up and the rivers shrank to just a thin trickle of water. The grass turned brown and died, and desert plants like sagebrush, mesquite, yucca, prickly pear, and the giant saguaro cactus replaced the greener, moisture-loving vegetation. Pinon, juniper, and other pine trees took over from the leafy trees in the mountain regions. Unable to survive without sufficient water and food, the giant beasts lumbered off in search of greener pastures. (Of course, many simply died of starvation and dehydration.) Gradually, the once pleasant meadows were transformed into a blistering desert.

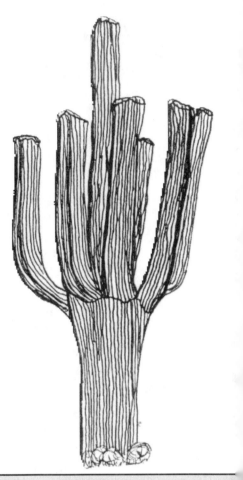

This giant saguaro cactus is 250 years old. is 50 feet tall and weighs about six tons.

But despite the disappearance of the big game, the hunters remained. They adapted to the changes in wildlife by shifting their sights toward the smaller game that was still available. They snared jackrabbits, squirrels, and birds in the nets they had fashioned from plant fibers. They even snagged lizards and snakes for their family dinners. To supplement the meat, the women and children gathered juniper berries, walnuts, cactus fruit (like that of the prickly pear), nuts from the pinon tree, and "rice grass" (a wild grain).

Like other early Americans, the people of the Southwest dressed in animal skins. Rabbit skins were especially valued, since they were so soft. Since rabbits are small, and one animal didn't provide very much fur, many of the timid creatures had to be caught. A woman skinned a rabbit by cutting the hide into a narrow circular strip, just as you might slice the skin of an apple.

The skin of one rabbit made a thin ribbon many feet long. About a hundred of these were needed to make a single man's robe. Imagine the work involved in that! The rabbit pelts were sewn onto cloth made from the fiber of the yucca plant. They were used for blankets as well as robes.

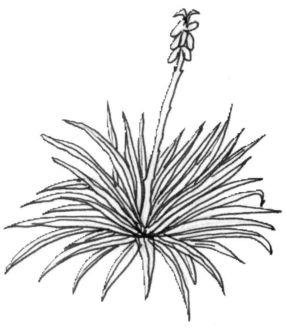

There were other sources of fur even smaller than rabbits. In a cave in Nevada archaeologists discovered an ancient blanket made from the skins of 600 meadow mice! Think of the amount of patience required to skin each tiny creature and then sew all the hides together onto the yucca cloth.

And indeed it was their patience and resourcefulness that enabled the desert dwellers to survive in a land of greatly diminished plant and animal life.

> Like the Mesoamericans, the dwellers of the Southwest made good use of the yucca plant. The tough, sinewy fibers of the spiny-tipped yucca leaves were used for making sandals, nets, mats, baskets, brooms, and brushes. Yucca fruit was served with meals, and the plant's roots (known as soapweed) made a fine lathery shampoo.

A CROSSROADS

Even as the Southwest became drier and hotter, nomads occasionally ventured there from neighboring regions. Some were simply pursuing game animals, while others came as traders. But whatever the reason for their arrival, these visitors often shared many of their own devices and designs with the local people. For example, hunters from the Great Plains taught the desert dwellers how to build a pit house. This involved digging a circular pit about two feet deep in the desert soil. The pit became the floor and lower walls of the house. The upper walls and roof were made with branches. A pit house was much more substantial than a simple brush shelter, and, like a cave, it had the extra advantage of being warm in winter and cool in summer.

Travelers from the Pacific Coast brought the technique for weaving baskets from plant fibers for the storage of seeds and berries. These could be woven so tightly that they could hold water. Then, by dropping hot rocks into a basket of water, a woman could raise the temperature of the liquid enough to cook a nutritious stew of meat, seeds, roots, and leaves.

From the north came an important innovation in weapons technology — the bow and arrow. Hunting with a bow and arrow was a lot more efficient than using the traditional spear, since a man could carry many more arrows than spears, and he could make a dozen shots in the time it would take him to hurl and retrieve his single spear. Also, a tightened bowstring (made of animal sinew) propelled an arrow with a great deal of force.

These new methods of building homes, making containers, and designing weapons certainly improved the quality of life for the desert dwellers. But by far the most significant innovation came from Mesoamerica.

CORN ARRIVES IN THE NORTH

In later centuries, descendants of the early inhabitants of the Southwest would tell stories of how their ancestors had emerged from a dark underworld and roamed the world until the gods taught them to cultivate the soil and grow corn. Actually, these "gods" were traders from Mesoamerica, who brought seeds of squash, beans, and, most particularly, corn (the wonder crop).

By about 1500 BC, farming had "caught on" in the Southwest, although it did not immediately replace the traditional hunting and gathering of food. The hot, dry conditions of the region were far from ideal for growing crops. Only the higher elevations received enough rainfall to make farming possible. And even there, the corn cobs that were harvested were so small that they made up only a fraction of the peoples' diet.

> Corn is the only food staple grown today in both the northern and southern hemispheres. Unlike rice, which thrives only in tropical climates, and wheat, which needs a temperate climate, corn grows everywhere — in virtually every part of the world where humans can grow crops! (All a farmer needs is sunshine and plenty of water!)
>
> Other grains, like wheat, produce six measures of seed for each measure planted, but a single kernel of corn yields 150 measures. This makes corn many times more productive than other grains.

By around 300 BC, three major cultures were emerging in the Southwest — the Hohokam (Hoh HOH kum), the Mogollon, (Mo GOH lon) and the Anasazi (Ah nah ZAH zee). Each had its own distinctive living patterns which depended upon the nature of the physical environment. People from these three groups knew about each other and often visited one another's settlements for purposes of trade, so there was a fair amount of exchange of ideas as well as products. They lived peacefully — archaeologists have found no evidence of battles. Everyone (except the chieftain and shaman) was considered an equal, so there were no sharp class distinctions. Each of these cultures thrived for over a thousand years.

THE HOHOKAM — INGENIOUS RIVER DWELLERS

The first fulltime farmers in the Southwest were the Hohokam, a Pima Indian word meaning "those who have gone before." They lived along the Gila and Salt Rivers in the flat Sonoran Desert of southern Arizona — near modern Phoenix and Tucson. (See the map on page 110.) The rivers brought abundant life to this parched land. They were teeming with fish and water-fowl, and the gently sloping riverbanks, shaded with willows and cottonwoods, attracted all sorts of thirsty game animals. Wandering tribesmen discovered this pleasant region when the surrounding landscape was changing from woodland to desert. Countless generations lived here as hunters and gatherers, gradually adapting to the rigors of the increasingly arid environment of sun, sand, and cactus.

Around 300 BC, the first efforts were made to grow corn along the riverbanks. Farming was no easy task in a place that received an annual rainfall of only four inches (mostly all at once) and where daytime temperatures often exceeded 100 degrees F. But the river dwellers made the barren land fertile and productive by building small irrigation canals. These carried water a few hundred feet from the rivers to the more distant parts of their fields. Possibly they learned about this concept from traders coming from Mesoamerica, or maybe they stumbled upon the idea by themselves. What's important is that the Hohokam no longer had to depend upon the desert's meager offerings of cactus, snakes, and lizards!

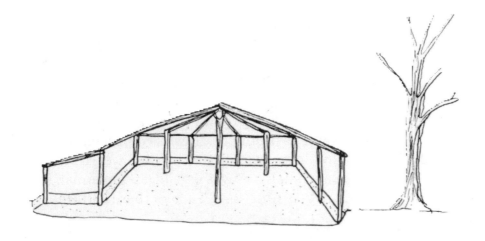

Cutaway of a Hohokam Pithouse

The farmers often built aboveground shelters near their pit houses to store their grain. Eventually, the idea of sturdy aboveground dwellings caught on, and many people abandoned their pit houses in favor of solid rectangular structures of stone or adobe clay with earthen floors. These proved as weather-proof (cool in summer, warm in winter) as the pit houses. As the population of a settlement grew, houses were built more closely together. In time, this led to the development of large, multi-chambered structures — a prehistoric version of our modern apartment houses. Each complex had special communal rooms set aside for storage and household chores like grinding grain. New units could be built beside or even on top of existing ones.

But the design of the old pit dwellings was never truly abandoned. It simply served a different function, one related to its original purpose. Since the earlier people had often buried their dead beneath the floors of their pit houses, those dwellings had long been associated with the spirit world as well as everyday family life. So when the shift was made to aboveground dwellings, sunken rooms (like small pit houses, but deeper) were dug in every village. They were

The Hohokam found the blossom of the saguaro cactus to be delicious. The sweet buds ripened in early summer and could be eaten fresh or dried for later. Sometimes they pressed the buds to yield a syrup that could be fermented. This produced a pleasant sweet wine. The blossom of the giant saguaro is the state flower of modern Arizona.

used for holding religious services and community meetings. The rooms were entered from a hole in the wooden roof by a ladder. Known as *kivas*, these subterranean rooms would play an important role in the lives of the people of the Southwest for centuries to come.

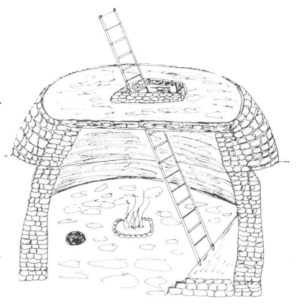

Cutaway of a Kiva

But let's get back to farming. The Hohokam mastered the techniques of irrigation and created a vast network of canals that covered thousands of acres. Their only tool was a long pointed digging stick. (Marks of the digging sticks have been found on the walls of canals uncovered by archaeologists.) The earth was carried off by teams of laborers in woven baskets. This was the most extensive water-control system north of Mexico in prehistoric times.

Some of the canals were 30 feet wide and 10 ten feet deep. The flow of the water depended upon gravity, and headgates constructed at canal forks allowed the farmers to divert or admit water as they needed it. The gates were made of tightly woven grass mats, backed by wooden stakes. They could be raised, allowing the water to flow freely under them, or lowered to hold the water back. The Hohokam even understood the process of evaporation and enlarged the carrying capacity of a canal by digging it deeper rather than making it wider. (It would have been much easier to make it wider, but a greater surface area would have allowed more water to evaporate.)

The canals enabled the farmers to grow two corn crops a year, one in the spring when the river swelled with melting snow from the mountains, and the other in late summer when heavy rains fell. (This was the one time when stormclouds made it over the mountains!) Irrigation also made it possible to grow cotton in the desert. (Cotton, another plant imported from Mexico, requires a great deal of water.)

The Hohokam diet centered around corn. The kernels were ground into flour (cornmeal) on *metates* similar to the ones used in Mesoamerica. The flour was often mixed with water and cooked in a ceramic pot to make porridge. To this could be added meat leftovers or greens, like wild mustard and rhubarb. Unfortunately, the stones used for grinding the corn took a toll on the people's teeth. A study of skeletons found in the region show that many suffered from gum disease. This is probably because part of the stone was ground into the flour, and when the people ate the porridge, the bits of stone (grit) slowly wore down the surface of their teeth. (The ancient Egyptians had a similar problem, and possibly the Mesoamericans did as well.) The skeletons also indicate that the women had well developed hands (from grinding the corn), while the men had strong upper arms (from laboring in the fields). A skeleton was discovered in a tomb that was taller than average and showed no evidence of physical labor. Since it was surrounded by luxury items, we can only conclude that this was an important (and inactive!) ruler.

> Around 200 AD, the people living in the Southwest began making clay (ceramic) pots to hold their food. These were far more practical than the old woven baskets. They kept the seeds fresh for longer periods of time and out of reach of pesky insects and rodents.
>
> The fragility and weight of the clay pots would have made it difficult to carry them from place to place. The fact that the people made so many of them offers proof that they had a more settled lifestyle than their ancestors.

The growing communities slowly took the first steps toward civilization, as individuals began to specialize in particular tasks. The farmers were clearly the most important people, since their labor produced the crops that kept everyone alive. But they depended upon the guidance of the local leaders, who oversaw the management and repair of the canals as well as mediating whenever conflicts arose among the local people. Priests devoted their energies to spiritual matters, while craftsmen produced pottery, cloth, and luxury items like jewelry. It was a good life, although certainly not an easy one by modern standards. Given the hard physical labor required of many and the lack of medical knowledge, the average person died by the age of forty.

The principal Hohokam town, known today as Snaketown, was continually inhabited from about 400 BC until 1000 AD. Like many of the other larger towns, it had a large oval ball court. Its playing surface was 165 feet long and about 63 feet wide — making it the largest of the courts yet excavated north of Mexico. Unlike those in Mesoamerica, the ball court had no hoops in the walls. The goals were designated by stone markers at either end of the court, as they are on a soccer field. While digging at the site, archaeologists discovered small clay statues of ballplayers, wearing shin and shoulder pads. They also found some balls made of raw rubber, a material that does not naturally occur in Arizona and must have been imported from Mexico.

The influence of Mesoamerica can also be seen in the earthen platform mounds, covered with adobe, that have been found at many Hohokam sites. They were fairly small (about ten feet in height). They were probably bases for temples.

The Hohokam certainly did owe a lot to their neighbors to the south — seeds of corn and cotton, the concept of a ball court, the design of platform mounds, and, possibly, irrigation technology. To this list we should add a number of luxury items that were imported by Mexican traders — copper bells, pyrite mirrors, and colorful macaws, which the Hohokam priests kept as pets and as a source of feathers for their ceremonial costumes. (And don't forget those rubber balls!) The Hohokam culture was, in fact, so greatly influenced by people living to the south that some archaeologists consider it the northern edge of ancient Mesoamerican society.

But Hohokam artists accomplished great things on their own. Artists decorated the landscape itself, chiseling or painting figures on canyon walls and boulders and inside caves. The paintings, done with mineral colors, are called *pictographs* ("picture writing), and the carvings are known as *petroglyphs* ("stone carvings"). Many of these still exist and tell us something about those early settlers. Hunting scenes provide evidence of their use of the bow and arrow (the Hohokam were the first people of the Southwest to use these weapons), so we know they ate plenty of meat with their vegetables. Images of groups of dancers holding hands suggest their outgoing community spirit. Ceremonial masks, human hands, and the figures of birds, insects, game animals, and snakes that appear frequently in the artwork provide clues about religious beliefs and practices. One strange-looking character — Kokopelli (the name given him by the Hopi Indians who lived in the Southwest long after the Hohokam) — is a humpbacked flute player. He was probably a fertility god of the Hohokam, although the Hopi regarded him as a clever trickster. (He appears again and again in Hopi myths in this role, and he has recently become a very popular cult figure in the Southwest, appearing on everything from sweatshirts to coffee mugs!)

Hohokam artists made pots by placing coils of wet clay on a small, mushroom-shaped clay anvil. As the potter turned the anvil with one hand, he shaped the vessel with his other hand using a wooden paddle. Then he painted human and animal figures as well as geometric designs, usually red against a tan background. In the later years, the designs became more intricate. The pots were fired in an earthen pit heated with a fire of dry twigs.

Kokopelli

Archaeologists were puzzled when they discovered many pots that had been deliberately smashed and buried with the ashes of cremated bodies. Possibly they were broken in order to release the spirits of the objects painted on them so that they could travel to the "next world" with the dead person's soul.

The human figures on the pots are "mini portraits" of the Hohokam people. They apparently wore loose-fitting cotton garments and sandals. Many wrapped their hair in headbands or turbans. They often painted, and even tattooed, their bodies. A few wore jewelry similar to that found in Mesoamerica — earrings, rings, bracelets, pendants, hairpins, and cheek (and even lip) plugs.

Hohokam stoneworkers carved bowls and incense burners in the shapes of people, lizards, and toads. Weavers produced cotton cloth on a back loom similar to the one used in Peru. (This design was probably another import from the south.) In later years, artists created beautiful things with seashells obtained from the Pacific and Gulf Coasts. Some of the shells were inlaid with turquoise and strung as necklaces. Others were etched with intricate designs by coating the surface with a protective veneer (probably acid-resistant pitch) and soaking the shell in a weak acid formed from fermented cactus juice. The acid ate away only at the parts of the shell that had been cut. The design could be seen once the coating was removed. Some of the etched shells date from about 1100 AD, which means that the Hohokams were the first people in the world to learn the art of etching. (A similar technique of etching was not discovered in Europe until the 15th century.)

In the second half of the 14th century AD, the Hohokam towns and villages were abandoned. No one knows for sure what happened. Some scientists believe large-scale flooding of the rivers could have demolished the unlined irrigation canals and caused a breakdown in the agricultural system. Others believe there was a terrible drought. Fortunately, the basic network of the Hohokam canal system survived, and a modern irrigation system has been virtually superimposed on the early one to divert water from the Salt River for the city of Phoenix.

THE MOGOLLON – MASTER POTTERS

While the Hohokam were flourishing in the southern desert, another culture, known as the Mogollan, was thriving in the mountains along the Arizona-New Mexico border. (They are named for a cluster of mountain peaks where many of them lived.) The Mogollon were not as sophisticated as the Hohokam, probably because they lived far from the major trade routes and had less interaction with peoples of other cultures. However, they did learn how to grow crops from the river dwellers.

As early as 200 BC, Mogollon farmers were harvesting corn, beans and squash in isolated mountain valleys. Their diet was supplemented by nuts and wild grasses (they had as many as 40 varieties of wild

> The Mogollon mountains were named after an 18th century Spanish governor. His nickname, Mogollon, means sponger!

plants at their fingertips) as well as the rabbits, beavers, muskrats, squirrels, turkeys, deer and bighorn sheep brought home by the hunters. In fact, given the enormous supply of wild plants and game, the crops grown by farmers made up a small part of the diet.

The families lived in clusters of pit houses that were dug up to four feet into the ground. These were similar to the earliest homes of the Hohokam. Each dwelling had a framework of logs — spruce, fir and pine — which supported a mud-plastered roof. It was entered via a long, narrow ramp on the east side (away from the prevailing wind). The pit house was ideal for the temperature extremes of the mountain valleys, where it could be 100 degrees during the day and near freezing at night. Branches burning in a central fire pit offered heat for cooking and warmth within the house, the smoke rising through a hole in the roof. Most villages had a central pit house, larger than the others, where the men met to smoke their clay pipes, to make tools, snares, and nets, and to hold religious ceremonies. It was similar to a Hohokam kiva.

Bighorn sheep, like the one above, lived in the high mountains rising above the desert. They could jump and climb easily in dangerous places. Elastic pads on their feet would grip the rocks and absorb the shock of the animal's gait as it bounded from peak to peak. They were very hard to catch, but sometimes the early settlers of the Southwest brought one home from the mountains for dinner.

Around 500 AD, several Mogollon hamlets sprang up in the valley of the Mimbres (MEM brays) River in southwestern New Mexico. It was much easier to farm in the river valleys than in the mountains, so many people flocked to this region. It would become the heart of Mogollon culture. As the communities grew, the farmers learned to irrigate their fields, thanks to a little help from their friends, the Hohokam.

The Mimbres are famous for the elegant and imaginative pottery bowls they produced. They were among the first people in the Southwest to fashion bowls out of clay, but it was not until about the 8th century AD that they learned from the Hohokam about the art of decorating them. Before too long, they were creating a quality of design unmatched by other cultures in the region.

Most Mimbres potters were women. Here's how one went about her task. First, she molded the wet clay from the river bed into coils and wound them to make a shallow bowl, smoothing and shaping the sides with her fingers. Once she had the basic shape, she scraped the sides with a stone or gourd and then applied a layer of pure white clay (kaolin) to the inside. Now the fun part began! Using brushes fashioned from yucca fiber that she had chewed until soft, she decorated the inside of the bowl. Carefully, she drew intricate designs of zigzags and triangles with the white, black and red paints she had made from dried plants and ground minerals. Then with a very steady hand, she painted parallel lines so thin that 15 of them could fit inside a border of less than an inch. At the very center of the bowl she drew a figure of an animal, such as a bird, bat, bighorn sheep, rabbit, lizard, or insect). Or she might paint a human figure. Once decorated, the bowls were fired in a primitive kiln made of large fragments of discarded pottery that were stacked under and around the new pieces.

> The Mogollon knew how to make most of the the knots we use today — the square knot, granny, slip, half hitch, and sheet bend knot.

Once again, the ancient artwork provides valuable clues about the people's appearance and daily life. The Mimbres villagers wore simple kilts made of plant fibers until traders brought them cotton seeds. For warmth, they made blankets from strips of fur or netted bird feathers. They fashioned sandals from yucca fibers, a material they also used to make nets and ropes. During leisure time, they played simple tunes upon reed flutes, gambled with wooden dice, and popped the dried kernels of corn on the cob in the glowing embers of the hearth. And, of course, they loved listening to a storyteller.(Doesn't everyone?)

Many of the Mimbres bowls were placed in a grave after they were ceremonially punctured or "killed" — each bowl had a hole punched through the bottom with some kind of sharp instrument. Perhaps, like the Hohokam, the Mogollon did this to release the spirits of the figures decorating it.

The culture of the Mimbres River Valley was at its height in the 11th century AD. Although it had a population of only 3,000, distributed in about a dozen villages, it was one of the largest cultures in the region. By this time, the people were living in multi-family structures of river stones set in a mortar of mud or adobe. Many of these complexes contained dozens of rooms. Yet, like the Hohokam, the people of the Mimbres maintained the tradition of the pit house in their underground kivas.

The Mogollon disappeared as a distinct culture sometime between 1200 and 1400 AD. Once again, no one knows why their way of life came to an end, but it certainly had something to do with a lack of food. We do know that the climate was extremely dry during this period, so their water supply would have been very limited. Many of the people migrated north into the mesa country, while others went south to Mexico. Wherever they went, they carried their traditions with them. The Zuni, who flourished in New Mexico in more recent times, were descended from the Mogollon.

> One bowl has a painting of two young men and monster. The figures have been interpreted by some archaeologists as the Hero Twins of Mesoamerica drawing rain from the mouth of a monster identified as Cloud Swallower, thus ending a drought. Like the Hohokam, the Mogollon apparently heard many things about the rich cultures to the south.

THE ANASAZI — CLIFF DWELLERS

The Anasazi settled in ancient times in the desert highlands in the Four Corners region (the junction of present day Utah, Colorado, New Mexico, and Arizona). This is a land of spectacular yet rugged beauty, dominated by towering red and yellow sandstone mesas and deep canyons. Four Corners is also an archaeologist's delight because of the large number of ancient sites found here. Their contents are well preserved due to the dry highland climate.

The Anasazi were great traders, as you will soon discover, and they developed one of the most extensive prehistoric cultures north of Mexico. Their traditions had a tremendous effect upon the lives of people living in most of New Mexico, northern Arizona, southwestern Colorado, southern Nevada, and much of Utah. This was indeed a vast territory, although it was not heavily populated — large areas of uninhabited land stretched between the villages that were built near a water supply.

> Anasazi means "the old ones" in the tongue of the Navaho people, who settled in the region many centuries later.

Many of the ancestors of the Anasazi sought shelter from the harsh winters and the summer extremes of temperature in the mouths of the caves that riddled many of the cliffs. Others built houses of sticks and mudbrick on the desert floor. They hunted deer and smaller game like rabbits, prairie dogs, gophers, rats and mice with spears (and, later, with bows and arrows). They learned to weave nets from yucca fibers to trap some of the smaller animals. One net has been found that is over 240 feet long and three feet high. It was made from almost four miles of carefully woven human hair and yucca fiber! It looks a lot like a tennis net. The hunters probably stretched the net across a narrow gully and beat the nearby bushes to chase the animals into it. The net was painted black in the middle so that the unsuspecting prey would mistake it for a hole and try to jump through it.

> The Anasazi later grew beans and squash with their corn. They planted the seeds of all three plants in a single hole. The squash would come up first, spreading out to provide ground cover that discouraged weeds. The corn would emerge next, its stalk shooting up through the squash and providing a convenient pole for the later-germinating bean plant to climb. After harvesting, the dried cornstalk was recycled as fuel. These three vegetables provided a healthy diet: an enzyme in the beans released the protein in the corn and made it digestible to humans, while the squash added minerals and vitamins.

The early Anasazi are also known as the *Basket Makers* because of the many containers they skillfully wove from yucca and milkweed fibers. The baskets came in all sizes. The biggest ones, intended for carting heavy loads, were carried on a person's back, supported by a woven strap slung across his forehead. Others fit the shoulders like our modern backpacks. Smaller baskets were designed to hold seeds and other dry goods. Some were covered with mud to make them extra water tight and to allow them to be placed on hot embers to cook the evening meal.

Even when they began to grow corn, most Anasazi continued to live in their cave shelters, often in shallow pit houses with thatched roofs. They built above ground granaries, first of mud-covered sticks and then of stone "glued" together with mud mortar. These storage units proved so sturdy and "weather proof" that some people built larger ones to live in. (Where have you seen this scenario before?) In time, most cave dwellers had abandoned their pit houses for the newer model.

> Like the Mogollon, the Basket Makers loved to play games with dice. A set has been found, complete with leather carrying bag. Some of the dice have carved sides, others have holes drilled in them. When thrown, the dice offer 44 possible combinations.

The first aboveground houses had walls that were thin and fairly crude, with stones of various dimensions set randomly in the mortar. But through trial and error, the builders learned to lay sandstone of uniform shapes in neat, tight patterns. Sandstone is a sedimentary rock (formed in layers). Piles of it were lying along the bases of the cliffs. Since each "slice" was naturally flat at the top and bottom, the builders only had to cut them into pieces to produce handy blocks. These building blocks enabled the Anasazi to make thicker walls that could support stout rafters and heavy roofs of brushwood and adobe. Ladders led up through hatches in the ceilings to the rooftop, which provided a pleasant, well-lighted workspace. (The hatches doubled as smoke holes.) The Spanish called these apartment complexes *pueblos,* their world for "village." Ever since, Native Americans living in this sort of dwelling have been known as Pueblo Indians.

By 900 AD, most Anasazi had left the protection of the cliffs and were living in apartment complexes of sandstone, adobe, and wood along the canyon bottoms or at the tops of mesas. More improvements in masonry (stone wall building) techniques enabled them to construct even thicker walls, which could support the weight of two or more floors. New apartment complexes were now built with stories that rose in stair-step fashion, so that residents could continue to make use of rooftops. So in the new apartment complexes, one room was built on top of another, and another on top of that. With each new level part of the roof of the apartment below became an outdoor workspace that was perfect for cooking, drying food, and painting pottery. Wouldn't this be a pleasant place to escape to from the darker living quarters?

Some of these multi-family dwellings contained as many as 300 rooms. They were usually built in the form of a crescent, fronting on a large open plaza (somewhat like the temple complexes of Mesoamerica). Although some homes had doors opening onto the plaza, the main means of entry was still through the roof openings, probably for security reasons.

Like the other peoples of the Southwest that we've learned about, the Anasazi gathered to discuss events or participate in religious rites in subterranean kivas. However, their kivas were deeper than those of other cultures, and they had special features, such as benches lining the walls. They were entered by a ladder that protruded through a hatch. People descended into the kiva facing the rungs of ladder — to look down was believed to shorten one's life! In the center of the large underground space (always lighted by a fire) was a small hole called the *sipapu*. This hole was believed to be a gateway to and from the spirit world. It also symbolized the entry through which the first people emerged onto the earth's surface.

Canyon walls offered huge surfaces for Anasazi artists to paint their pictographs and carve their petroglyphs. Let's take a look at their self-portraits. By modern standards, the ancient people of the Southwest were rather small (most of the men were just over five feet tall), slender, and tan-skinned, with thick coarse black hair, dark eyes, and little facial or body hair. Anasazi men wore their hair in three braids, and the women often wore their hair up, held in place with cactus combs and bone ornaments. A woman's long hair was sheared off after she died to yield materials for nets and other useful items. (This was considered her special gift to the living.)

Like the other people of the Southwest, both genders wore a cotton kilt most of the time, and they protected themselves in cold weather with cloaks of rabbit skin. Some cloaks were woven of human hair and cactus fiber. For religious ceremonies, the priests often wore cloaks of turkey feathers. (The Anasazi had flocks of tame turkeys to provide feathers as well as meat). The most important article of clothing was the sandal, woven from yucca fiber. It protected the feet from rocks, cactus, and hard-shelled insects.

Anasazi mothers strapped their babies to hard wooden cradle-boards while they were working. (Anasazi babies never knew the joy of a playpen!) The boards could also be worn as backpacks when the mothers worked in the fields. Since the babies' skulls were soft, they became flattened in the back. As a result, every adult Anasazi had a flat-backed head. This seemed very normal to them, and strangers who hadn't had the same childhood experience probably looked a bit strange. (Do you remember how the Moche purposely molded their babies' skulls for a "cone-head" appearance?)

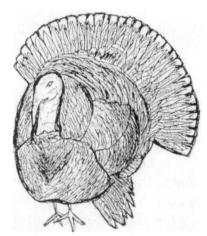

The Source of Those Turkey Feathers!

Recently, archeologists have found that the Anasazi of 1,400 years ago wore sandals with soles so well designed they're the technological equivalent of modern day Nikes and Adidas. Two hundred of their yucca sandals, finely woven by artisans using 22 different textile techniques, were discovered in 1930 by Earl Morris, archaeologist. The sole's inner and outer surfaces displayed different patterns, and knotting on the underside may have furnished traction on wet surfaces. For much of the next half century, the sandals languished in a drawer at Arizona State Museum in Tucson until Kelley Hays-Gilpin, an archaeologist at Northern Arizona University, studied them for her dissertation.

That project led to a book PREHISTORIC SANDALS FROM NORTH-EASTERN ARIZONA. Hays-Gilpin studied the safety literature used by modern shoemakers and found that the Anasazi sandals measure up favorably. The soles have the perfect tread depth for gripping, and the edges point out so that water squirts away, as it does with modern tires. The soles have multi-directional ridges to reduce slipping, and the yucca gives them flexibility. The Anasazi had deer, badger, and elk to kill, so they could easily have relied on leather moccasins, but they didn't — they preferred these open sandals.

This discovery led to the development of a product that became "all the rage" throughout the West and beyond — the Teva sports sandal. In 1996 the University of Utah hosted an exhibit of Anasazi sandals, sponsored in part by the company that makes Tevas. Its opening was blessed by a Navajo medicine man.

When a teen aged Anasazi girl became eligible for mar riage, the custom was for her to sit by the door of the home of a boy about her age for four days, grinding corn. Every time the boy left his house he would see her and watch her grind the corn. If, after the four days, he decided that he liked the way she did the job, he would marry her! As a wedding gift, he would weave her a pair of yucca sandals and put them on her feet. His parents would give the young couple a blanket of turkey feathers.

Of course, the Anasazi ate lots of corn. Their favorite recipe was hominy — cornmeal cooked in water, often with some pieces of turkey or rabbit mixed in. A special treat was the meat of the mountain sheep. (Killing one of these animals provided the hunter's family not only with tasty meat but a wooly hide for blankets and cloaks.) A favorite beverage was made from sumac berries sweetened with the juice of the fruit of the prickly pear cactus.

Like the other primitive people you've been learning about, the Anasazi believed the animals they killed, like the crops they grew, were gifts from the gods. A hunter would laid head of an animal he had slain on a pillow of pinon boughs and cover its body with a blanket of turkey feathers. Then he placed prayer sticks around it. (Prayer sticks were pieces of wood that had been carved and decorated with paint and feathers) He offered prayers to the animal's spirit, pleading for forgiveness for killing it and thanking it for offering its life so he could feed his family.

Chaco Canyon

For centuries, communities of Anasazi lived happily in secluded clusters of dwellings, separated by mountains and deserts but linked by trade and religious traditions. Around 1000 AD, however, many people began to settle in Chaco Canyon in northern New Mexico. The canyon is actually a huge gorge about 22 miles long and several miles wide in some places. The flat expanse below the canyon walls seemed a good spot for farming, but there was very little water in the Chaco River that flowed lazi-ly through the canyon floor. And there wasn't much rainfall — only about 20 inches a year — and most of it came during short, sudden downpours. So the farmers experimented and eventually figured out how to channel the runoff that cascaded down the cliffs after a storm so it could be collected in catch basins. The water was then diverted to the low-lying fields through a system of canals and head gates. This irrigation system enabled them to produce abundant harvests and attracted many other settlers to the canyon.

By 1050 AD, there were more than 5,000 people living in Chaco Canyon. Huge living complexes were constructed along the valley floor, each of them connected to the others by well-made roads. There was plenty of food, thanks to the irrigation projects, so many craftsmen were able to create all kinds of wonderful objects. From 1100 until 1300, the communities of Chaco Canyon formed the center of a rich culture that spread to hundreds of villages scattered across the desert basin. This was the "Golden Age" of Anasazi culture.

> Recently, an estimated 540,000 gallons of water flowed down one side of the canyon. If captured in a basin, this could water a huge number of plants for a very long time!

Pueblo Bonito ("Beautiful Village" in Spanish) was the largest and most spectacular of the complexes of this period. It was, in fact, the largest single dwelling ever built anywhere up to that time. Almost twice as wide as a football field and longer than two football fields placed end to end, the multi-structure of family apartments and government suites rose four and five stories high and contained 800 rooms. Over a million stones went into its construction. Several large kivas were sunk into the two central plazas, while dozens of smaller ones were scattered among the apartments. Two of the largest kivas, each about 63 feet across, could hold several hundred inhabitants. Their roofs were supported by massive interior pillars. The kivas were reached through subterranean entryways.

Pueblo Bonito was built in the shape of a D. The straight part, which served as a protective wall, faced south towards the Chaco River, while the curved section, containing the living quarters for about 1200 people, was tucked against the cliffs of the canyon. For reasons of defense, there were no windows in the front on the lowest level, and none at all on the crescent side. The only means of entry was by ladders, which could be pulled up by those inside. The rooms of the crescent were built on a series of graduated terraces. Windows looked out onto the terraces and toward the central plaza below. The sandstone of the outer walls of the complex was covered by a smooth coat of plaster, parts of which were decorated with brightly painted designs. (These decorations have not survived until modern times.) There was little furniture in the rooms. The people slept on grass or yucca mats, but they spent most of the day outside.

PUEBLO BONITO IN CHACO CANYON

Pueblo Bonito was the heart of Chaco culture, but there were nine other complexes nearly as large scattered along the canyon floor. They had an average of 216 rooms apiece, with small kivas for about every 30 rooms and usually one very large kiva.

Huge numbers of logs were used as floor and roof supports in these "Great Houses." Archaeologists estimate that about 215,000 trees had to be felled for this purpose with stone axes. The nearest forests were over 50 miles away. It was no small task to haul them back to Chaco Canyon, but the job was made easier by the starburst of roads that spoked in many directions from the entrance of the canyon. The roads stretched to distant points as far as 90 miles away. They were unerringly straight. In fact, the builders were so determined to avoid turns that instead of going around a mountain, they carved steps that rose steeply up the side. A traveler probably used a combination of wooden and rope ladders and scaffolding to get up the sheer part of a cliff, and then continued along the road at the top. Getting down the other side must have been equally challenging.

Chaco merchants traveled great distances to trade local products, such as pottery, cornmeal, and jewelry, for luxury items. The most sought after items were sea shells from the Gulf of California, macaws and copper bells from Mexico, and turquoise from New Mexico. Actually, turquoise played a huge role in the Chaco economy. The bluish-green stone was often used as money, and it was displayed as a sign of wealth. Recently, a tomb was uncovered in the canyon that contained more than 500,000 pieces of turquoise, many of them fashioned into beads and pendants.

> Pueblo Bonito's designers understood passive solar heating and cooling techniques. The thick masonry walls, pierced by only a few small windows and doors, moderated Chaco's wildly fluctuating temperature, keeping the rooms comfortable in the stifling summer heat of day and the chill of night. Facing south, the complex was stepped down from rear to front, creating rooftop terraces and giving each level the maximum benefit of the winter sun.

At Canyon de Chelly in northeast Arizona, archaeologists discovered the grave of an old man curled in a fetal position, his graying hair pulled back in a ponytail. He wore a cloak made of golden-eagle down and two cotton blankets, one of which, despite its age, looked brand-new. A single ear of corn rested on his chest. Around him were a large, powerful bow and a single wood-tipped arrow, five pottery jars, and four woven baskets containing pinon nuts, beans, salt, and cornmeal. Think about how much the burial this one old fellow tells us about Chaco culture. The most amazing part of the find was a huge amount of cotton yarn, wound in thick skeins. There were more than two miles of it! Beside it lay a wooden spindle (used to spin cotton into thread). Why was there so much cotton in the grave? Was this man a highly regarded weaver? And why the spindle? Did the people who buried him believe that he would spend eternity weaving cloth?

A number of mummified bodies have been uncovered in nearby caves, complete with hair and dehydrated flesh still adhering to the bones. One of these, currently in the American

Museum of Natural History in New York, was wrapped in a turkey feather blanket and hundreds of yards of cotton cloth. (Does all this buried remind you of the ancient people of coastal Peru? It should!)

The dwellers of Chaco Canyon, like all Anasazi, worshipped the life-giving powers of the sun. They greeted the morning sun by offering a pinch of cornmeal, which they threw upon the ground. Mothers held their newborn babies up at dawn to receive the sun's blessing.

The priests made careful note of the place on the horizon where the sun's first rays appeared. Since this point shifts during the year, moving north as the days grow longer in the spring, their observations of the position of the sun helped them to calculate the best time for planting crops. The priests also observed the moon and the stars, and they used their findings to create a calendar. Each month began with the crescent moon, and the days to the next new moon were recorded by cutting notches into a stick. Carved symbols on these "calendar sticks" indicated the dates of special ceremonies.

The priests also built structures with specially placed windows to observe the heavens and predict the solstices and equinoxes. The most important religious ceremony took place at the winter solstice. It marked the middle of the year, the time when the sun would slowly begin to light the sky for longer periods of the day. (Two of the small corner windows of Pueblo Bonito lined up with the sun's position on the winter solstice.)

> The farmers in some regions used the sun's rays to increase the yield of their crops. Here's how. They aligned stones in a grid stretching across their fields. The dark stones retained the sun's heat into the night, warming the nearby plants and extending their growing time.
>
> Some of the squares of the grid were filled with gravel to help trap rainwater and runoff, which could then be used to water some of the plants.

> On July 4, 1054, the advent of a supernova (known as the Crab nebula) was marked by a stellar explosion of great magnitude. It remained visible in the daylight sky for over for three weeks and at night for almost two years. We know this great event was observed by the Anasazi because of the discovery of a reddish brown pictograph on a sandstone wall in Chaco Canyon. It consists of a hand, which may indicate the sacredness of the spot, a star, and a crescent. Below these symbols is a depiction of the sun — three concentric circles around a dot.
>
> The arrangement of these figures closely resembles what actually occurred that July morning in 1054 — the star (the supernova) appeared south of the crescent moon, with the sun below the horizon. Even the moon's crescent phase for the day (its tips pointing to the west) has been confirmed by computer analysis.

The Chaco culture collapsed around 1150. Perhaps the growing population used up all the available timber for building and firewood. Or perhaps the canyon dwellers were attacked by nomads. We know that raiding parties of Navajos and Apaches were invading the area from the north at about this time. But most likely it was a drought that signaled the end to this rich culture. Between 1276 and 1299 almost no rain fell. Scientists know this by studying tree rings in the beams of the ruins. How could the people grow their crops with no water? What we do know is that by 1300 all the settlements of the canyon had been deserted.

The Hopi, descendants of the Anasazi, claimed that the people left the canyon because a serpent deity — a god of rain

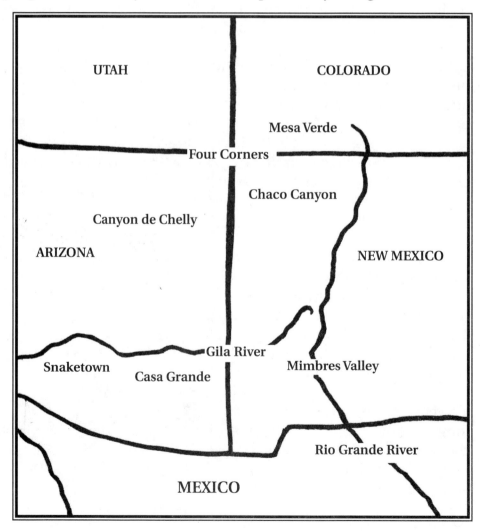

and fertility — had abandoned them. Helpless without their god, the people traveled south until they reached a river, where they built new pueblo villages and started their lives anew. (This is, in fact, just what they did.)

Mesa Verde

During the 12th and 13th centuries, bands of Anasazi built villages of stone buildings in the cliffside crevices of mesas in southwestern Colorado. Their ancestors had lived on the fertile mesa tops, where they grew corn, squash, and beans. There was sufficient rain at that altitude to water the crops. But around 1200 AD, their settlements shifted to the more sheltered sites in the cliff face. Why? Maybe because they needed to use every bit of available space on the mesa top for farming, or perhaps they were worried about being attacked by enemy tribesmen.

The cliff dwellings could be reached from the valley floor only by an arduous climb using toeholds hacked out of the rock. (Imagine climbing straight up a vertical cliff with only small holes to fit your feet into and to place your fingers in for balance!) To get to the top of the mesa where they grew most of their crops, the cliff dwellers used similar toeholds and, whenever possible, ladders, which were placed on small jutting ledges. Men and women (many with babies on their backs) climbed up the cliff each day to work in the fields. Harvested vegetables were carried down to the dwellings in baskets strapped to the men's backs. Climbing up and down took great skill and courage, especially since the canyon floor lay 700 feet below the mesa top!

A major site of cliff dwellings was *Mesa Verde* (MAY sa VAIR dee), which means "Green Table" in Spanish. It was named by the European explorers for the dense pinon and juniper forests growing on its flat summit. Like those of Chaco Canyon, the buildings of Mesa Verde were constructed in tiered steps, so that the roof of an apartment formed the front porch of the one above it. All the units of a single complex looked out onto a central plaza, which served as the focus of daily life. The rooms were low and narrow — they must have been rather cramped. At the period of greatest prosperity, the villages built in the cliffs of Mesa Verde were home to 7,000 men, women, and children.

Cliff Palace was the largest of the complexes. It had over 217 rooms and 23 kivas. Living in such a large multi-structure had many advantages. There were plenty of community activities and everyone felt safe from enemies prowling about below. But the cliff dwellings presented some major health problems. Since they were confined to fairly narrow ledges, human waste and other refuse was often deposited close to the living areas. This created a breeding place for harmful bacteria that cause disease. Approximately half of all children born at Mesa Verde died by the age of four. And the dampness of the stone dwellings posed another theat — a large number of adults developed crippling arthritis.

At one time certain Anasazi were cannibals! Human remains dating from the 12th century have been found in southwestern Colorado that appear to have been systematically dismembered, defleshed, and stewed, leaving the bones in the same condition as those of animals used for food! Patterns of burning suggest that many of the bones were roasted over a fire while still covered with flesh.

Archaeologists link the cannibalism with violent conflict between the desert communities during a time when the Chaco culture was in collapse and there was a terrible drought.

Then the droughts hit — for 24 years there was little or no rain. Little by little, groups of families climbed down to the valley floor and set out in search of new homes. By the dawn of the 14th century, Mesa Verde was a ghost town, the pueblo complexes left to crumble. Some of the cliff dwellers found refuge in the deserts and built new villages around oases, where spring water seeped out of the layers of sandstone. Others traveled south to the banks of the Rio Grande River and built new multi-family complexes there.

The Zuni people (the descendants of the Mogollon) had a myth about the abandonment of Mesa Verde. It tells how a giant, called Cloud-swallower, consumed the "cloud-breaths" of the gods, which were the source of moisture from the sky. Snow ceased in the north and the west, rain ceased in the south and the east. The mists of the mountains and the waters of the valleys dried up. Then the twin gods of war destroyed the evil giant. But fearing that the water would never again freshen the fields, the cliff dwellers fled away to the south and east. Only those who had perished during the drought remained, "dried, like their cornstalks that died when the rain stopped." And those dried remains have lasted all these years to provide us with clues to some of the the mysteries of Mesa Verde.

This certainly isn't the end of the story of the American Southwest. Although the three ancient cultures you've been learning about abandoned their homes for one reason or another, their descendants continued to thrive in that bleak and barren land. You'll learn all about the Hopi and Zuni, as well as other cultures like the Navajo and Apache, in the next volume of this series.

But for now, let's look back at the Hohokam, Mogollon, and Anasazi. Do you see any patterns? All three groups were farmers, although the Hohokam had to work the hardest to grow their crops in the desert. All three learned to build multi-family living complexes and maintained the traditions of the pit house in specially designed rooms, usually underground, where men could gather to communicate with the gods or to discuss more worldly matters. Each culture took advantage of the clay that is so abundant in that part of the world to produce many practical, and often beautiful, pieces of pottery. All believed in an afterlife, and even though war might have been a concern, there is no evidence of fighting and bloodshed. What other patterns can you see?

Mesoamerica had an effect of varying degrees upon the communities of the Southwest, but everyone living there certainly benefited from one import from the south — corn, the wonder plant. Can you imagine large communities of contented families living in the Southwest without corn? Surely not. So isn't it fitting that the farmers of this region should have passed on some of their seeds to others? In the next chapter, you'll learn about how people living to the east not only learned to cultivate corn — some of them created the first civilization north of Mexico.

REVIEW QUESTIONS

1. Describe the geography of the American Southwest.
2. Where did the people of the Southwest first grow corn?
3. What new use did the desert dwellers find for their old pit houses, once they started living above-ground?
4. How did the Hohokam water their crops?
5. What are four ways in which Hohokam culture was influenced by

Mesoamerica?

6. What's the difference between a pictograph and a petroglyph?

7. Who was Kokopelli?

8. Why did several Southwestern cultures smash their pots before burying them?

9. How did the Hohokam craftsmen etch designs on the seashells?

10. How did the wealthy Hohokam people dress?

11. What are the Mimbres people most famous for?

12. Where is the Four Corners region of the United States?

13. Where did the first Anasazi seek shelter?

14. Describe the Anasazi apartment complexes.

15. Why did the Anasazi have flattened heads?

16. Describe Chaco Canyon.

17. What stone did the Anasazi of Chaco Canyon use as money?

18. Describe the Anasazi calendar.

19. Why did the people of Mesa Verde move down from the mesa top to the cliff-side caves?

20. Why did the Anasazi abandon Mesa Verde?

PROJECTS

1. Study a detailed map of the geography of Mexico and the American Southwest. Find the area around modern Mexico City, where many ancient cultures once flourished. Now look at the regions of Arizona and New Mexico where the Hohokam, Mogollon, and Anasazi lived. After carefully examining the terrain, point out several possible routes traders from Mesoamerica might have taken to share their wares with the desert dwellers living to their north. Share your findings with your classmates.

2. Around 1300 AD, certain groups of Hohokam merged with other local cultures. During this period *Casa Grande* (Spanish for "Big House") was built. This multistory structure rose rises 35 feet above Sonoran Desert. Find out more about this building and its purpose. Then write a short report.

3. Find out more about the pottery of the Mimbres Valley. Make a poster showing the designs and decorations of the pottery.

4. Make a clay model of a typical pueblo complex or of the dwellings of Mesa Verde.

5 THE MOUND BUILDERS

When the glaciers retreated at the end of the Ice Age, the eastern third of North America was covered with dense forests alive with game animals — rabbits, squirrels, woodchucks, opossums, raccoons, turkeys, deer, elk, moose and bears, to name just a few! Unlike the Southwest, where everything dried up, this part of America remained a land of plenty. It received just the right amount of rainfall — not too much and not too little. Rivers and lakes were filled with bass, bowfin, catfish, and many other kinds of fish. The trees were incredibly large. Since there was no one to cut them down, they simply grew and grew until they died of disease or were struck by lightning. The upper branches formed a thick, green canopy that let in only occasional bursts of bright sunlight. Every fall, the forest floor was littered with edible nuts — acorns, chestnuts, walnuts, pecans, and hickory.

Most of the nomads who wandered into the eastern woodlands liked what they saw and stayed. (Wouldn't you?) They built huts from sticks, branches and bark, and they helped themselves to the abundant plant and animal life. Sometime around 2000 BC, some of the women figured out that by putting sunflower and squash seeds in the ground they could grow new plants. In time, many families were adding roasted squash and sunflower seeds to their dinner menus.

Sunflowers

Many people settled along the rivers, since fish could be caught any season of the year. Also, the waterways enabled them to travel to other areas to hunt or trade. Over the centuries, the population of river dwellers dramatically increased, until distinct cultures emerged among them. The three most important were the Adena, the Hopewell, and the Mississippians. The Adena appeared first. They were eventually eclipsed by the Hopewell, who were, for some time at least, contemporaries of the Mississippians. This last culture was by far the richest and most sophisticated of the three, and it lasted the longest.

All three cultures produced some wonderful works of art and established large trading networks. But what most distinguishes them are the thousands of earthen structures they left behind. That's why they're known as the Mound Builders.

THE ADENA — EARLY MOUND BUILDERS

The first Adena settlements appeared in the pleasant Ohio River Valley around 900 BC. Why the name Adena? Because that was the name of a town in Ohio where their remains were first uncovered.

The early settlers were farmers as well as hunters and gatherers. They cleared their land using a method known as "slash and burn." Here's how it was done. After removing fallen branches and other brush, the men sliced a strip of bark around the trunk of each tree. This caused a tree to eventually die, since water and nutrients could no longer circulate between its roots and leaves. The next year, the dead, dried out trees were set afire, leaving the area cleared and ready for planting squash and sunflower seeds. As an added bonus, the ashes fertilized the soil.

Building a home in the forest was fairly easy, since materials were so plentiful. The Adena houses were constructed upon a circular framework of wooden posts that were lashed together with cords of plant fiber. The walls, which tilted slightly outward, were often covered with mud, and the entire structure was topped with a steeply pitched thatched roof. In the center of the clay floor was a hearth, where the women cooked the food and the family gathered for warmth. "Kitchen equipment" included pottery jars made by coiling clay, wooden bowls and spoons, seed containers fashioned from dried gourds (squash), and ladles made from turtle shells. The dwellings of an extended family —

the homes of the older parents and of their sons (and their wives and children) — were clustered around the fields.

The Adena were the first woodland people to link the villages scattered across a wide area through a network of trade. Merchants traveled great distances — far beyond the Adena villages — to obtain raw materials. They paddled their canoes north to Lake Superior to obtain copper nuggets, south to North Carolina to trade for sheets of mica (mica is a mineral that separates into thin, tough, and often transparent layers), and to the distant Atlantic and Gulf Coasts for seashells. They brought these materials back to the Adena crafts-

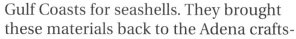
A Typical Adena Dwelling

men, with whom they traded for finished products. Then they packed up their new acquisitions and headed off for "foreign" markets once more. Thus, the cycle repeated itself, again and again.

Adena artists fashioned the metal, stone, and shells into beautiful ornaments and jewelry. The women concentrated on making more practical items, like cooking tools and clothing. Lacking any kind of loom, they used their fingers to plait and twine the threads of grass and plant fibers to make cloth, bags, mats, and sandals.

The early Adena had an interesting way of preparing their dead for burial. Mourning relatives would lay the body of a loved one on a scaffold and leave it on a hilltop until scavenging birds had stripped the skeleton of all flesh. Then they gently placed the bones in a shallow grave. As communities grew larger, bodies were simply buried (intact) in the earth. And it became the tradi-tion to bury the body of an important member in the floor of his own house. After being sprinkled with powdered red ocher and decorated with strung shells, the body was placed in a pit in the floor. (Possibly the ocher was intended to give the colorless flesh a more lifelike appearance. Or maybe the color red was associated with the spirit world.) After a religious ceremony, the house was burned down, and its ashes were covered with thin layers of different types of dirt — each with a different mineral content and therefore a slightly different shade of brown. The wide range of hues came as quite a surprise to archaeologists when they excavated these sites!

In later years, bodies of leaders were placed in clay-lined tombs made of carefully cut logs. These were covered with many layers of dirt, just as the ashes of the houses had been. The earliest burial mounds found in the eastern woodlands date from about 500 BC. In later centuries, the log tombs became larger and more elaborate, and the mounds grew quite large.

Archaeologists have discovered many interesting artifacts within the burial mounds, including a number of stone tablets engraved with birds of prey. These probably symbolized the birds that stripped the flesh of exposed dead bodies in earlier times. Sometimes a death mask, embedded with animal teeth and bones, was placed upon the face of the deceased. One body held a polished skull on its lap, perhaps the head of a vanquished enemy! Another was buried with no fewer than 32 stone pipes carved in the shapes of humans and animals. He was either a wealthy fancier of stone pipes or a well-respected carver.

Pipes were among the most treasured possessions of the Mound Builders, as they were of many other cultures. Stone pipes in North America date back to 2500 BC. The early tribesmen smoked 27 different plant species — from shredded willow bark to goldenrod flowers to tobacco. The smoke was associated with fire, a sacred element, and thus was considered a purifier. It rose to the heavens and made contact with the spirits.

When someone was sick or injured, the medicine man, or shaman, filled his tubular pipe with some sort of plant and lit it. He either puffed on the pipe and then blew the smoke on the injured area or, if the person was ill, he inhaled the smoke and then dramatically exhaled it as if to disperse the disease.

Many of the other burial objects were carved with a curious symbol — an eye in the palm of a hand. Did this represent the soul of the deceased safe in the hand of death? Or did it symbolize the "all-seeing" power of the spirits of the afterlife? Perhaps you have a better explanation. There are so many mysteries associated with the ancient peoples of America, and we can only guess at the meanings of much of what we find.

The bodies buried in the log chambers tended to be taller than ordinary people — some were as tall as six feet, which was very unusual in those days when the average man's height was about five feet. (Remember how the buried leaders of the Southwest were also very tall? Why do you think the leaders might have been chosen from among the very tallest men?)

As new graves were added the a mound, hundreds of thousands of basketfuls of specially selected and graded types of earth were piled up and tamped down above and around them. The bodies of ordinary people, curled up in round clay basins, were often placed randomly in the dirt as the mound grew. The Cresap Mound in West Virginia contained the skeletons of at least 54 people. One of the largest existing mounds, in Miamisburg, Ohio, was at least 68 feet high before excavators (foolishly)

> A headdress made from the skullcap and antlers of a deer was found in one tomb. It was probably worn by a shaman (whose grave this was) to impersonate the animal during a religious ritual, such as to summon the deer's spirit before a hunt.

skimmed off part of the top in 1869. Some of the mounds were surrounded by great circular earthen enclosures. They are known as the "sacred circles." Religious ceremonies were probably held within the walls.

As the Adena influence spread, more mounds were built along the rivers. It has been estimated that there were once between 300 and 500 sites in and around Ohio. Unfortunately, many of the mounds have been destroyed by natural events (like floods) and by farming and other human activities. Some were simply removed to make way for new farmland or paved parking lots and shopping malls.

The Adena also built mounds in the shapes of men and animals — bears, foxes, tortoises, and birds. One huge mound constructed in the shape of an eagle had a wingspread of 240 feet! Another was a 150-foot long man with two heads and arms stretched wide. (No one has figured out the meaning of this odd, two-headed fellow. Can you?) The most famous of the animal mounds is the great Serpent Mound in southern Ohio — a huge earthen snake five feet high, 20 feet wide, and 1, 254 feet long. If uncoiled, the snake would stretch for a quarter mile! It seems to

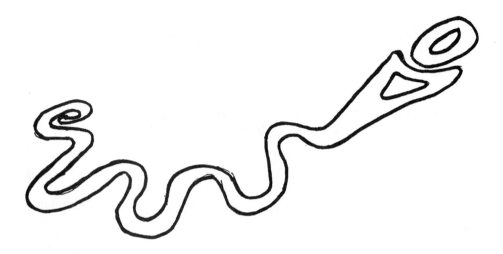

The Serpent Mound

slither across a ridge, its open jaws grasping an oval object, possibly an egg. (What could the egg symbolize?) Or is it a creature of the deep gobbling up a human soul? And why a snake? (Have you noticed that, like the Mesoamericans, many people living north of Mexico thought about snakes and birds in spiritual ways? (Do you think that snakes are mysterious or scary? Did you ever wonder about why birds fly? Ancient people did, all the time!)

We can easily look at these animals in pictures taken from airplanes. But imagine how difficult it must have been to build them when the designer could not stand back to view the workers' progress. (The Mound Builders faced the same problem as the creators of the Nazca lines. Both cultures succeeded in creating gigantic figures, but we're still wondering how they did it!) And what was the function of the animal mounds? Since no human remains have been uncovered in them, we know they were not tombs. Most likely they represent the totems, or special animal spirits, of particular villages. And since they can only be properly viewed from the heavens, they were probably intended to be seen and appreciated by the gods.

The Adena people lived happily and productively until about 100 BC, when their culture was absorbed by a newer one, known as the Hopewell. As you will see, these two groups had much in common.

The Serpent Mound was one of first conservation projects in the United States. It was discovered in the middle of 19th century when a tornado mowed down the forest that had long kept it hidden. Farmers wanted to remove the mound and plant their crops where it stood, but some society ladies in Boston frantically sent out newsletters about the danger the snake was in. They raised enough money from concerned citizens that they could buy the mound and have it preserved as a national monument.

THE HOPEWELL – MASTER CRAFTSMEN

The Hopewell culture originated in Illinois and spread to Ohio. Eventually, its influence ranged over much of the North American continent east of the Great Plains. (The name "Hopewell" comes from the owner of a mound-studded farm in Ohio where many artifacts were discovered.)

The Hopewell held elaborate religious ceremonies, and especially lavish burial rites. This resulted in even bigger mounds than those of the Adena. They also produced some of the best art in ancient America north of Mexico. Everything about the Hopewell seemed to be bigger and better than what had gone before in the eastern woodlands.

The earliest Hopewell dwellings were circular huts built of flexible young saplings set in the ground and then bent over to form a rounded roof. The roof was covered with animal skins, tough sheets of elm bark, or mats of woven fiber. A hole in the roof vented the smoke from the fire pit dug in the packed-clay floor. In later years, larger and sturdier homes were built, often in geometric shapes — squares, ovals, and rectangles. Although the villages were larger than those of the Adena, each one never had more than a few hundred inhabitants, most of whom were related.

The villages emptied in late autumn and early spring, when everyone set out to forage in the forest to build up their stocks of food for winter or (in spring) to replenish them. The hunters used spears as well as snares to trap deer and smaller animals. The land had such rich resources that the Hopewell devoted little time to farming, although they did grow some squash and sunflowers. The women preserved much of the meat the hunters brought home by smoking it (in closed smokehouses) or drying it on racks set up outside the houses. Corn (the wonder crop) was introduced by traders from the Southwest, but it produced such small ears that it was set aside for special religious festivals.

Hopewell potters decorated their pots and jars with intricate geometric figures and bird designs and then fired them in a hearth. They also made interesting clay statues of their kinsmen. Other artisans produced finely woven mats, while stoneworkers made sharp obsidian knives and cut thin sheets of shiny mica in the shapes of animals and people. Jewelers worked with tortoise shell, bone, animal teeth, and quartz to fashion necklaces, bracelets, and earrings. Thousands of freshwater pearls were gathered from the Scioto River in Ohio to decorate clothing or fashion jewelry. Artists carved the fossilized tusks of long extinct giant mammoths that they discovered in the dirt. (They even carved human bones, which have turned up in some of their ancient tombs!) Sculptors carved pipes from soapstone in the shapes of birds, forest animals, and people.

Hopewell women wore calf-length skirts of woven plant fibers in the warm weather, while the men wore breechcloths made from the same material. Young children wore nothing at all in the summer. In winter, everyone kept warm beneath robes of animal fur. The women wore their hair in long braids, and the men shaved their heads (probably using bear fat and an obsidian blade), except for a topknot, which could be clipped short or braided. For special occasions, both men and women wore jewelry.

> Everyone enjoyed playing games. A favorite was the cup-and-pin game, which involved trying to flip a bone into a conical bone cup fashioned from a deer's hoof. The bone was attached to the cup with a piece of animal sinew. (Our modern version is a rubber ball attached by a long string or elastic to a plastic cup.)

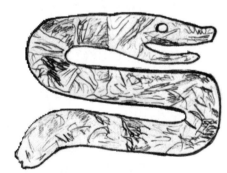

A Snake Fashioned from a Single Sheet of Mica

The Hopewell were the finest metalworkers of their time, crafting tools and ornaments out of copper and, occasionally, silver and gold. But their preferred metal was copper. They never learned to smelt the metal from copper ore (this means melting the copper out of the rocks) as the ancient Egyptians and Greeks did — they used almost pure copper nuggets. They produced a sheet of copper by alternately heating and hammering a nugget over a hot fire. When the sheet had been hammered into its desired thinness, the coppersmith cut out a variety of ornaments, such as headdresses, breastplates, ear spools, beads, pendants, panpipes, and statues of birds and fish.

An Eagle Talon Cut from Mica

To obtain the raw materials they needed for their artwork, the Hopewell extended the trade network of the Adena. Merchants traveled throughout eastern North America, including much of Canada, and westward into the Rocky Mountains. (Their trade routes covered two thirds of the present United States!) Merchants traveled in large dugout canoes. Some were 25 feet long and four feet wide, requiring a crew of six to paddle them. The boats were made from oak logs, which had been split and then and hollowed out with a smoldering fire and stone gouges.

A Trumpeter Swan of Turtle Shell

The traders exchanged their cargo of Ohio pipestone, flint, freshwater pearls, crafted tools and ornaments for copper around Lake Superior, blue flint in Indiana, chalcedony in North Dakota, silver in Canada, obsidian and the teeth of grizzly bears in the Rocky Mountains, mica in the southern Appalachian Mountains, and alligator teeth, barracuda jaws, seashells and turtle shells along the Atlantic and Gulf Coasts.

Most of the artifacts we have were found in burial mounds — and the Hopewell built thousands of them. In fact, many of the greatest art objects were apparently made specifically to be buried with the dead, rather than enjoyed by the living. (We know this because of their unused, or "mint," condition. The same was true of the cloth buried in ancient South American tombs.)

The Hopewell mounds were huge (up to 40 feet high), and they were often enclosed within earthen embankments, far grander than those of the Adena. Sometimes small mounds in the shapes of circles, squares, octagons, and even animals, were built within the embankment. The shapes may have been the totems of different clans, or perhaps they had a more mystical meaning. At the site in Ohio for which the Hopewell culture was named, 38 conical mounds were built within an enclosure covering 110 acres. Another complex at Newark, Ohio covered four square miles and contained many burial mounds, a great effigy mound of an eagle, circular earthworks, and a two and a half mile-long corridor linking the mounds to the banks of the Licking River. (The modern residents haven't shown the Hopewells much respect. Much of the Newark site now lies within a golf course and a fair ground!)

Let's take a closer look at one of the burial mounds. Deep within was a log mortuary house containing several chambers — one holding the body of a person of high rank. The other chambers were filled with objects for the afterlife — some useful, most pricy "baubles." Around the body lay the remains of people of lesser importance. Scientists examining the Hopewell skeletons have discovered that many of the leaders had arthritis in their elbows, perhaps as a result of hurling many spears. (The leaders were also of above average height. Where have you heard about this before?) Many of the people of lesser rank had arthritis of the wrist, which suggests the repetitive hand movements of certain craftsmen. (This is an ancient version of the wrist problems modern Americans can develop from using a computer mouse!) Generally, though, the Hopewell appear to have been healthy, and they had few cavities in their teeth.

A dead leader was buried with everything he needed to "show off" in the next life. Archaeologists have also discovered necklaces, bracelets, and ear ornaments made of gold, silver, copper, pearls, and shell. Other artifacts included polished stone pipes carved as people and birds, silhouettes cut from sheets of pounded copper and mica, and even engraved human bones.

Many clay figurines were smashed before being buried. Perhaps, as with the pots of the Southwest dwellers, they were smashed to liberate the spirits of the figures for the afterlife. Some tombs contained huge quantities of raw materials — freshwater pearls, copper, mica, tortoise shell, and silver. Why do you think these unworked objects were placed in the graves?

The interior log vault of one mound held the skeletons of four adults, lying side by side. At their heads were the remains of two infants. (Their children?) Accompanying them was a profusion of objects made from copper, mica, silver, and tortoise-shell as well as thousands of pearls. (Could the pearls have been a kind of currency?) Why did they all die together? Once again, no one is certain, but perhaps modern technology can test their DNA to determine their relationship.

Another grave contained the remains of a young man and woman laying side by side. Both bodies were adorned with necklaces of grizzly-bear teeth, copper ear ornaments, copper breastplates, and unusual copper nose pieces. Around the skeletons of the woman were thousands of pearl beads and copper-clad buttons of wood and stone (possibly history's first buttons). She was buried wearing a magnificent pearl-beaded mantle, the fabric of which had long since disintegrated. Nearby was a copper ax weighing 28 pounds. (How could anyone wield an ax as heavy as this? Or was it placed there as a symbol?)

> Some mounds were so massive that American settlers of the 19th century wondered whether they were forts built by a "lost civilization!"

At Mound City in Ohio there remain 23 mounds. Buried in one of these was a hoodlike headdress made from pieces of animal hide (probably a wolf) joined to the front of a human skull. This was a mask worn by the priest who was buried there. The same tomb contained hundreds of pipes, copper figures of birds, turtles, and humans, and a copper-covered wooden carving of the poisonous death cup mushroom. Another tomb held many tools and raw materials, which suggested that it marked the grave of a talented artisan.

About 400 AD, for reasons unclear, the Hopewell culture was in decline. Perhaps this was due a change in climate (scientists know that it turned much colder for quite a long time) or a surge in the population. Both of these happenings would have diminished the supply of food. The bow and arrow had recently been introduced into the region, replacing the less efficient spears. Did this lead to the over-killing of game or, perhaps, to an increase in warfare? Whatever the cause of the decline, the trading network fell apart and no more mounds were built. When white settlers arrived in Ohio in the 18th century, they found the local natives living in very humble huts amid the earthworks of the once great Hopewell people.

This figure, known as "birdman," was engraved on a piece of Hopewell jewelry. Does it remind you of the feathered warriors of Mesoamerica? Do

But the Mound Builders didn't die out with the Hopewell. The traditions and beliefs of those ancient people lived on among the inhabitants of other parts of North America. The people living along the Mississippi River built upon the accomplishments of other culture groups to create the most advanced prehistoric civilization north of Mesoamerica.

THE MISSISSIPIANS — PYRAMID BUILDERS

Mississippian culture took root around 700 AD in the flood plains of the lower Mississippi Valley. It gradually spread until it engulfed a huge chunk of land — stretching from Canada south to the Gulf of Mexico and from the Rockies east to the Appalacian Mountains.

The key to the success and prosperity of the Mississippians was the corn they grew. Remember how the corn grown by the Hopewell produced very small cobs? That early variety also needed a long growing season of 200 or more days, so it was only planted in the most southern regions. Given its relative scarcity and the small size of the cobs, we can undeerstand why the Hopewell set it aside for special occasions. But in about the 8th century AD everything changed, when new strains of corn were imported into the eastern woodlands from the Southwest. These produced larger cobs (and therefore more kernels) and required only 120 frost-free days until they could be harvested. This new variety of corn could be planted farther north, while the southern farmers could count upon two harvests every year. Corn was no longer considered a luxury — it became the staple food for thousands of Mississippians.

The farmers planted the corn kernels together with the seeds of beans and squash in the furrows dug in a field. When the plants began to grow, the bean plants (which are climbers) twined around the stalks of corn, while the squash (which are creepers) spread their tendrils along the ground, choking out weeds and providing shade that kept the earth moist. It was a wonderful example of "plant teamwork." (The descendants of the Mound Builders would call these plants the Three Sisters.) The crops thrived in the rich soil along the Mississippi River and its tributaries, providing plenty of food for an ever-growing population.

Corn, however, was the most important crop. In fact, it was so essential to the lives of the Mississippians that they developed a cult to worship the sun, whose warm rays coaxed the seeds to sprout. Local chieftains performed special rituals to assure that the sun would shine. Because of their apparent power to control the daylight, they received a portion of the corn harvest as a form of tribute (like a tax). They stored some for use in their own households and distributed the rest to the general population. This way, everyone, farmer and craftsman alike, had plenty to eat.

Despite the influence of Mesoamerica upon the Mississippians, the river dwellers never developed a form a writing — that critical step in the development of a great civilization.

The plentiful food supply made it possible for some people to specialize fulltime in particular tasks, and Mississippian society gradually split into distinct classes. We've seen this pattern again and again, haven't we?

Sometimes a chieftain became greedy and picked a fight with a neighboring village or town. He could always count upon the aid of his warriors, who were eager to improve their social standing by demonstrating their bravery in battle. (The Mississippians were far less peaceful than the people of the Southwest.) Whoever won the dispute was entitled to a periodic tribute of crops, goods, laborers, and even land from the losing side. In this way, many leaders gradually extended their domains to include villages dozens of miles away, and they became quite rich in the process. At its peak (between 1200 and 1500 AD), Mississippian culture flourished in thousands of towns and hundreds of small cities. This is the closest the Mound Builders came to rivaling the great civilizations of Central and South America.

The ruling classes loved to show off their wealth on special occasions. They painted their faces and put on ornate headdresses, earrings, necklaces, arm and leg bands, and capes made from turkey feathers. At home, they surrounded themselves with beautifully carved statues and highly glazed ceramics. Their love of luxury encouraged the growth of a trading network that was even more vast than that of the Hopewell. Merchants traveled up and down the rivers, stopping at trading settlements established along the river banks to bargain for exotic raw materials — everything from mica to alligator teeth.

> As perhaps you've noticed, wild turkeys were tamed and raised by people living in many parts of America, from the eastern woodlands to Mesoamerica. They provided delicious meat, and their feathers were used to stuff pillows and to make attire such as capes and ceremonial robes — and even underwear!

> Even more that the Adena and Hopewell, Mississippian culture seems to have been greatly influenced by Mesoamerica. Traders from Mexico often ventured along the Gulf Coast and then up the Mississippi River, carrying many traditions north along with their products. As you read along, look for connections between the Mesoamericans and the Mississippians.

Like the Maya, the Mississippians believed that the universe was made up of three worlds. The harmonious *Upper World*, symbolized by eagles, falcons, and other soaring birds, was ruled by the nourishing spirit of the sun. The chaotic, watery *Under World* was associated with scaly, cold-blooded creatures, like snakes and alligators, that often lurked just beneath the surface of the river or marsh. Between these two regions was *This World*, the realm of humanity.

Turn back to page 43 and reread the paragraph about the Mayan view of the universe. Do you think the Mayan beliefs were carried north, or did the Mississippians simply look at the world in a similar way without ever hearing about Xibalda? These are the kinds of questions that make ancient history so intriguing!

Can you guess how we know so much about the Mississippians? That's right! Most of our knowledge comes from what they buried in their tombs. For example, a conch shell engraved with a cross within a circle seems to symbolize the Upper World — each arm of the cross representing one of the four cardinal directions (north, south, east, and west), and the circle being the sun, or perhaps the heavens themselves. Other engravings depict a warrior with a falcon eye, perhaps to associate him with the spirit of that powerful bird of prey. Some warriors are shown with wings, similar to the Hopewell "birdman" on page 126. Even a feathered serpent turns up from time to time in Mississippian art.

One interesting symbol that appears again and again is the weeping eye. Was it intended to express sadness upon the death of the loved one? Or do the tears suggest a plea for rain? (Remember the weeping rain gods of Mesoamerica?) Another common symbol is an open hand with an eye or a cross in the center of the palm. The "eye in the palm" was common among nearly all cultures of Mound Builders, but how would you explain the cross in the palm? (Think about the Mississippian view of the Upper World.)

> The Mississippians worshipped peregrine falcons and other birds of prey as spirit protectors of their warriors. An engraved gorget (a pendant worn over the throat) shows warriors with talons, winged capes, and birdlike tails descending from their waists.
>
> Could it be that warriors went into battle dressed like this, or do the birdlike attributes simply symbolize the warrior's special powers? What do you think?

Nowhere is the influence of Mesoamerica more evident than in the earthworks of the Mississippians. Unlike the Adena and the Hopewell, who constructed mounds primarily for burial, the Mississippians built truncated pyramids as bases for temples, council houses, and even the homes of important people. A typical pyramid had steeply sloping sides and a stairway of logs leading to its flat top. But while the Mesoamericans faced their pyramids and built their temples with stone, the mounds of the Mississippians were entirely earthen, and the structures on top were constructed of wood and thatch. Did the river dwellers lack the knowledge of quarrying stone, or did they wish to retain the earthen quality of the monuments of the earlier Mound Builders? No one knows for sure.

> Since the pyramids were not used as tombs, conical mounds similar to those of the Hopewell were constructed for burial of the wealthy. The bodies of ordinary people were buried in shallow graves in public cemeteries.

The temples atop the pyramids were forbidden to all but the priests and the guardians who tended the sacred flames night and day. Their interiors were decorated with strands of pearls, pendants of copper and shell, and headdresses of dyed turkey feathers, all of which were suspended from the rafters. (Perhaps the priests wore these during rituals.) On an alter stood painted wooden and stone statuettes of high-ranking departed ancestors. They were seated with folded legs, their hands on their knees, mouths half-open, and eyes wide as though they could see things that the living cannot.

> The temple fire was considered a reflection of the sun. Its guardians faced death if they let it go out!
>
> The Romans had a similar idea. Priestesses, known as the Vestal Virgins, kept the fire going in the hearth of the temple of the goddess, Vesta. If they let it go out, they were buried alive!

CAHOKIA

The greatest city of the Mississippians was Cahokia. It was built outside modern St. Louis, Missouri, just south of where the Missouri and Mississippi River come together. The city was connected to the Mississippi by a narrow channel that has since dried up. The site was named Cahokia after the natives who were living in the area when the French arrived there in the 17th century. As with most of the ancient sites, no one know this city's original name. At its height (around 1200 AD), Cahokia had a population of about 30,000 people, making it the continent's largest prehistoric settlement outside of Mesoamerica.

The city covered nearly six square miles and contained 120 mounds, many of them higher and broader than any others constructed by the Mound Builders. These included both conical burial mounds (conical in shape) and truncated pyramids with buildings on their flat tops. In fact, Cahokia was — and still is — the largest collection of pyramids ever constructed in one place anywhere in the world, including Egypt.

At the city's center stood a huge, multi-terraced pyramid mound covering almost 19 acres. This was the largest mound north of Mesoamerica, and the third largest structure in the Americas at that time. (It was surpassed by only two temple pyramids in Mexico.) It's base covered more area than that of ancient Egypt's famous Great Pyramid. The mound rose in steps to four broad terraces, reaching a height of 100 feet. It is known as Monks Mound after the French Trappist monks who planted vegetable gardens and fruit trees on its southern slopes in the 19th century.

Excavations of Monks Mound reveal that it was built in 14 stages, beginning around 900 AD and achieving its final form three centuries later. During all those years, thousands of workers lugged baskets of dirt from nearby "borrow pits" until the structure contained about 22 million cubic feet of earth. On the flattened top stood a rectangular wooden temple with a steeply pitched thatched roof. It measured 100 by 48 feet and towered more than 50 feet. On a lower terrace were the residences of the city's ruler.

Monks Mound Today

Monks Mound overlooked a great central plaza of about 40 acres. Most of the time, the plaza was a marketplace and community gathering spot, but on special occasions it became the site of religious processions and festivities. In the early spring (planting time) and late fall (harvest time), footraces and ritual dances to appease the gods took place there. Musicians kept the beat for the dancing with hollow log drums and gourd rattles.

Bordering the plaza were smaller mounds and clusters of wooden dwellings. Some of the platform mounds were bases for temples, while others were the sites of the homes of the most prominent people. The higher one's house, the more lofty his social status (and, of course, the closer he was to the heavenly spirits).

In addition to what they left behind in their tombs, the Cahokians passed on many clues about their culture to their descendants, the Natchez. They carried on their traditions long after Cahokia had disappeared. (European explorers observed and wrote about the "peculiar" lifestyle of the Natchez in the 18th century.) We know that the city's ruler was known as the "Great Sun." He was the earthly counterpart of the heavenly sun. For important occasions he wore a crown of white feathers topped with small red tassels and decorated with white seeds. (The crown, of course, symbolized the corn plant.) The Great Sun's foot never touched the bare earth — servants carried him everywhere on an ornate litter! He was advised by an upper class that included the Lesser Suns (his relatives and other nobles). Priests belonged to this class.

At the next level were the Honored Men and Women — the military leaders and the master craftsmen and master traders (and, sometimes, their wives). Then came the bulk of the population, the commoners. These were the workers, farmers, and warriors who provided the manpower to keep Cahokia functioning smoothly. Below the commoners were the slaves. They were either prisoners of war or acquisitions made by the wealthy elite at local slave markets. The slaves performed the menial tasks, like digging ditches and hauling baskets of dirt for mound building.

The higher classes referred to the commoners and slaves as "Stinkards." But despite their lowly status, the Stinkards were not doomed to living in obscurity. This is because the noble women were required to marry them! (Why? Perhaps to add "new blood"

> The Cahokians obtained salt from the waters of nearby salt marshes. Archaeologists have unearthed thousands of fragments of broad, flat clay vessels in which the brine was evaporated over open fires.
>
> Why salt? Perhaps the Cahokians needed to add taste to the bland plant food that made up most of their diet. (They ate little meat.) But one city couldn't have used that much salt, so some of it was probably put aside for trade.

to the elite classes in order to avoid the birth defects commonly caused by the intermarrying of related families.) Although a Stinkard did not rise in social status by such a marriage, his or her children did. A Stinkard could also move up one social level (becoming an Honored Man) by exhibiting bravery on the battlefield.

The houses of Cahokia — from the smallest huts of the Stinkards to the roomy homes of the wealthy — were all built of closely placed upright poles interlaced with reeds and cane. Their steeply pitched roofs were of thatch. The inside walls were covered with mud plaster to help insulate the house against extremes of weather, and those in the larger homes were sometimes painted red, black, or blue. Each dwelling had a hearth for warmth, but most cooking was done outdoors or in a separate shed.

Near the central plaza was a 100-foot-long playing field for a popular game known as chunkey. To play chunkey, two contestants running abreast down the field hurled eight-foot wooden poles at a rimmed stone disk that was bowled ahead of them down a court. The player whose pole landed closest to where the disk stopped rolling scored a point. Spectators gambled enthusiastically on the outcome. Unlike the ball games played in Mesoamerica, the losers did not pay with their lives!

A tall stockade fence (a palisade) of foot-thick logs set close together protected the heart of the city. Outside the fence were more houses and more mounds. Here and there were the borrow pits — the excavations that supplied earth for building the mounds. These were often filled with water and became scenic ponds. Beyond the outer ring of houses were about a dozen outlying villages, and beyond them were over 50 farming communities stretching for a dozen miles along both sides of the Mississippi River.

The stockade was rebuilt several times over the centuries because the wood had rotted. Rebuilding the fence involved cutting and carrying thousands of logs, placing them upright in deep trenches, and then plastering them with clay mixed with grass. It

> Several statues of chunkey players, holding their distinctive stone disks, have been unburied in Cahokia.
>
> Early European travelers left accounts of watching the Natchez (descendants of the Cahokians) playing chunkey. They were amazed to observe that the games sometimes lasted all day!

was a massive project. Built at intervals of about 80 feet along the fence were ramparts (towers) from which archers could defend the inner city by shooting arrows down on their enemies. The gateway was shielded by an L-shaped projection of the fence. This forced an attacker to approach the entrance from the side rather than head on. This not only slowed him down but exposed him to the fire of archers standing above on the ramparts.

But who was the enemy? Did the Cahokians fear neighboring societies or tribesmen living beyond the river shores? Or were the elite worried about a rebellion among the Stinkards who sustained their pleasant lifestyle? Once again, no one has the answer.

Just outside of the area of the stockade was a configuration of huge red cedar posts set in a perfect circle around a central observation post. The circle measured 410 feet in diameter. From a central observation point, priests could sight along the posts and line them up with the rising sun at certain times of the year (the equinoxes and the solstices). Perhaps they used them to determine when to plant corn and when to expect the annual river floods. Archaeologists call the circle "Woodhenge" after Stonehenge, a ring of huge stones (called megaliths) set up in ancient England to track the shifting seasons by observing the sun. The Cahokians built at least four of these circles (at the same spot) at different times — perhaps improving upon their calculations each time.

The leaders and high priests of Cahokia were buried within the stockade. Upon the death of a member of this class, the body was conducted up the ramp of a pyramid to its funerary temple by a line of mourners. There it was placed in a cedar litter and prepared for burial. The face was painted red (with ocher) and the entire body was adorned with jewelry of copper, mica, and pearls and enveloped in feathers and furs. The litter was then taken to a nearby conical mound or a lower terrace, where it was buried. If the deceased was a Great Sun, some of his attendants and even family members were sacrificed to join him in the afterlife. They were rendered unconscious by ingesting a potent plug of tobacco and

> The Egyptian pyramids had burial chambers at the core, so they were tombs. Mexican pyramids, with one exception, had no burial chambers but, instead, they had shrines at top, so they were temples. Mississippian mounds were a combination of both.
>
> Perhaps they were first built as tombs (like those of other Mound Builders), and then the temple was added at the top, as result of the influence of Mesoamerica.

then strangled with a cord placed around the neck. The Mississippians were the only Mound Builders that we know about who performed human sacrifices.

One mound contained the bodies of three important people who died at different times. One, a male about 45 years old, lay on a carpet of 20,000 conch-shell beads. His body was surrounded with grave offerings — rolls of copper, baskets of mica, and hundreds of arrowheads. Near him were pits containing the skeletal remains of attendants who had clearly been sacrificed. One of the pits held the bones of four men whose heads and hands were missing and whose arms were linked. No one is certain what this signifies. Another pit held 53 freshly strangled women between the ages of 15 and 25 and six male retainers. One thing is certain — the leader intended to have a lot of company (and attention) in the afterlife!

> Another way for a Stinkard to rise in social status was to sacrifice a member of his family at the burial of a ruler. Believe it or not, this was commonly done!

MOUNDVILLE

Cahokia's greatest rival, appropriately known as Moundville, was built on a plateau along the Black Warrior River in Alabama. When Cahokia began to lose its luster around 1250 AD (for reasons unknown, building projects ceased and the population declined), Moundville became the major Mississippian settlement. It was considerably smaller than Cahokia, covering only 300 acres and having a population of only 3,000. Its trade and influence extended over only about 240 square miles. But still, Moundville was a pretty impressive place for those early times.

> In some Mississippian tombs, archaeologists have found effigy jars of clay shaped like the heads of enemies of the deceased — their eyes closed and their mouths sewn shut. What do you think these signify?

The city's 20 mounds, varying in height from three to 23 feet, were arranged in a circle around a great plaza. As in Cahokia, some mounds were for burials, while others (the pyramids) were for temples and the residences of the nobility. One of these homes had seven rooms — an impressive number for that time and place. Moundville also had a large chunkey playing field. Outside the circle of mounds were two larger pyramids, one rising 60 feet and containing four million cubic feet of earth. A stockade surrounded the central area. Outside it were three large borrow pits that were filled with water and stocked with fish. In outlying areas were smaller villages with single mounds. The surrounding forests appeared almost "park-like" to the first Europeans who viewed them. The local people kept them that way by burning back the underbrush.

Many burial sites have been unearthed in and around Moundville. What is most curious is that much of the art seems to reflect a mood of brooding and sadness. For example, there is a face devoid of all features except eyes, which are weeping. Is this an expression of mourning, a prayer for rain, or did the people sense that their way of life was coming to an end?

THE END OF AN ERA

Cahokia slowly faded into oblivion. At first it simply reverted to an ordinary village, but by 1500 it had been abandoned altogether. By that time, the other cities, including Moundville, had also declined. Only a few pockets of Mississippian culture lingered here and there along the river valleys.

Once again, we must ask what happened. Did the population grow too dense, creating health risks, such as the communicable diseases associated with poor sanitary living conditions? Malnutrition apparently resulted from a diet of mostly corn, which is high in carbohydrates but low in protein and certain amino acids. The remains of the people exhibit an increase in tooth decay, anemia, and tuberculosis. Perhaps the final straw was a climatic change that brought on a famine. (Some scientists have theorized the opposite scenario, namely that the rising water table made much of the farmland along the river too wet to cultivate sufficient crops.)

Fortunately, as you've learned, many of the Mississippian traditions were passed on to their descendants, the Natchez, who lived in the Lower Mississippi Valley. You'll learn about them in Book II.

Only a few decades ago, archaeologists discovered the ruins of a society of mound builders that predated the people we've studied in this chapter by many centuries. In 1500 BC, a site in Louisiana known as Poverty Point was a major crossroads of trade for the entire Lower Mississippi Valley. Its name comes from the 19th century settlers, who considered the site a poor spot for a plantation. Yet, in ancient times this was the largest and most prosperous settlement in North America! It might have been an outpost of the Olmecs or another Mesoamerican culture.

Poverty Point was basically a sprawling complex of earthworks — a semicircle of six concentric ridges (four to six feet tall and between 50 and 150 feet wide) that were spaced about 100 feet apart. This arc of ridges stretched for almost 3/4 of a mile. Houses were built on top of them. Behind the ridges was a spectacular bird-shaped mound measuring 640 feet by 710 feet and rising 70 feet above the surrounding land. Outside the settlement stood ceremonial mounds, the largest standing 70 feet high and measuring 800 by 700 feet at the base. It has been calculated that these mounds contain 20 million 50-pound basketloads of earth!

This place was certainly ahead of its time, anticipating the widespread building of mounds in the eastern woodlands by at least 500 years!

REVIEW QUESTIONS

1. Compare the eastern woodlands to the Southwest.
2. What were the three main cultures of the Mound Builders?
3. How did the early Adena bury their dead?
4. How did the Adena burial sites evolve into mounds?
5. What do the remains found in the Adena tombs tell us about the social groupings of the people?
6. Describe the serpent mound of the Adena.
7. Why did the Hopewell have such a vast trading network?
8. What were some of the crafts of the Hopewell? (Name three.)
9. How did the Hopewell construct their mounds?
10. What kinds of materials were buried with wealthy Hopewell people?
11. How did Mississippian farming differ from that of the Hopewell?
12. What were the three "worlds" of the Mississippian? (Think in terms of religion.)
13. Name four ways in which the Mississippian culture was influenced by that of Mesoamerica.
14. How big was Monks Mound?
15. What was Woodhenge?
16. How was chunkey played?

PROJECTS

1. Make a map indicating the locations of the Adena, Hopewell, and Mississippian cultures. Be sure to indicate the waterways used for trade.

2. Find out more about the animal-shaped mounds of the Adena and Hopewell. Then check out the huge animal figures created on hillsides by pre-historic people in England. Write a report, comparing the figures of Americans and Europeans.

3. Find out more about Stonehenge. Compare it to Woodhenge in a report.

4. The ancient Egyptian tomb of "King Tut" can be compared with a Hopewell burial mound. Find out more about the Egyptian tomb and then write a report noting the similarities and the differences between it and the American one.

5. Make a model of Monks Mound. Study drawings of how it appeared in ancient times. Include the appropriate wooden structures on the top and lower terraces.

6. The Dickson Mounds make up a 162 acre site in Illinois. They include the remains of 251 Mississippians who settled there around 1100 AD. The skeletons, left as found, were put on display in a museum built to protect the site, along with the pots, tools, and other objects uncovered there. In the early 1970s, Native Americans in Illinois began to demonstrate for the remains to be reburied, out of respect for the spirits of the dead. Local residents differed, arguing that the exhibit taught others about the rich culture of the Mississippians.

   This issue continues to be debated, and laws have even been passed requiring certain artifacts and human remains to be returned to the ancestors of the dead. (In 1990 Congress passed the Native American Graves Protection and Repatriation Act.) As for the Dickson Mounds, activists entered the exhibit in 1991 and shoveled dirt onto several of the exposed graves. The following year the state of Illinois ordered the museum's burial exhibit to shut down.

   Although legislation has been passed to protect artifacts and remains and to return them to descendants of the buried if they exist, many people, especially those who run museums, believe that these objects should be in the public domain. In the late 1990s there was considerable protest about objects from Central and South America on display in the Boston Museum of Fine Arts.

   Find out more about this controversy. After examining the arguments, come up with your own conclusions about what should be done. Express your views in a report.

6 THE FAR NORTH AND THE NORTHWEST COAST

By now you've learned quite a lot about the waves of immigrants who crossed Beringia and then ventured south until they reached a warmer climate. But there were those who remained in the frigid wasteland of the Arctic, while others thrived in the rugged clime of the Subarctic. Still others settled along the cool and rainy Pacific coast that stretches from Alaska to Washington and Oregon. Conditions were not favorable in any of these regions for herding or farming, so the people had to live off the land. That wasn't an easy thing to do in these challenging environments of ice, tundra and soggy seacoast. In this chapter you'll discover how the people of the north carved out a good lifestyle among the most difficult of circumstances.

THE ARCTIC

The Arctic lies at the top of the world, stretching across the northernmost sections of North America, Europe, and Asia. It includes many islands (the largest being Greenland) and is bounded by the Pacific, Arctic, and Atlantic Oceans. This is certainly one of the most desolate places on earth. During the coldest months, the temperature dips to 60 degrees below zero in some places, and winds howl relentlessly across the endless expanse of snow. The sea itself turns to ice. To make matters worse, the sun never even rises above the horizon for three months in winter — the only light comes from the moon and stars, the northern lights (the *Aurora Borealis*), and the glimmer of twilight on the southern horizon. (The darkness occurs because the earth is tilted away from the sun at that time of year.) Surprisingly, the Arctic receives so little precipitation (less than ten inches a year) that it is classified as a desert! Some parts are drier than the vast Sahara Desert in Africa. The snow that does fall remains on the ground all winter long. How could it possibly melt in those cold temperatures?

> The name "Arctic" is derived from the Greek word *arktos*, meaning "bear." It is a reference to the constellation Ursa Major, or Great Bear, which appears prominently in the northern sky.

But relief does come to this inclement land. After the months of darkness, the sun slowly climbs higher and higher above the horizon until, for the three months of summer, it never sets at all! This explains why the polar region is often referred to as "the land of the midnight sun." The warmth of the summer sun melts much of the snow, transforming the icy landscape into a vast tundra of flat, brown plains. The water cannot drain into the earth because everything below the topsoil is permanently frozen (it's called *permafrost*), so it forms a maze of streams, marshes, and ponds. All too soon, the standing water is infested with buzzing mosquitoes.

> The permafrost of the Arctic often extends to a depth thousands of feet below the surface of the ground!

Little by little, the brown tundra turns green as the low-growing plants come to life. There is an astounding variety of them — 500 kinds of mosses, 2,500 types of lichens, 900 species of shallow rooted flowering plants, and scattered patches of short-rooted scrub bush and dwarf willows. By mid-summer, millions of tiny wild flowers carpet the tundra with bright colors — yellow, purple, red, and orange. There are no trees (the roots can't penetrate the permafrost), so the only wood is the driftwood that washes up along the shores.

Just as bountiful as the seasonal plant life in this land of extremes are the animals. The northern rim of the American continent has a rich array of sea mammals — killer whales, walruses, seals, and sea lions — as well as shellfish and cold water-loving fish like cod, halibut, salmon, and herring. Polar bears thrive in the coldest of times along the shores and ice packs, feeding mostly upon seals. Arctic foxes will wait patiently until a bear satisfies his hunger and moves on. Then they eat what's left of the seal carcass. Heavy-coated musk oxen, like the one in the figure to the right, munch upon whatever dormant twigs they can find sticking above the winter snow and dream, perhaps, of the coming spring. (The deep, dense wool of the musk ox, called *quivut*, is the most valuable raw fiber in the world today.)

A Musk Ox

In the warmer months, herds of caribou move up from further south to graze upon the plants growing on the tundra, while hibernating creatures like grizzly bears awaken to hunt for ground squirrels and other small animals. The summer marshes attract birds of prey, like owls and hawks, as well as huge numbers of migratory waterfowl — ducks, geese, and even swans. Winged insects fill the air, while spiders and beetles scurry across the ground. Those pesky mosquitoes can drive humans and animals insane. Even the caribou and musk oxen suffer from the relentless insects. Fortunately, the thick coats that protect them during the long winter also help them survive these maddening onslaughts.

As winter approaches, the herbivorous mammals and many carnivores of the Arctic put on extra layers of fat. The caribou acquires an amount of fat that is equal to one sixth of its body weight! The fat serves as an energy reserve as well as insulation. Sea mammals, like the seal and walrus, have a very thick layer of blubber.

Fur-clad nomads were probably thriving in the Arctic as long as 18,000 years ago. But the most important migration of Arctic dwellers came later from Asia by boat — long after Beringia had disappeared beneath the surface of the sea. They began arriving along the American coast around 3,000 BC. With a lot of determination and ingenuity, they created a viable way of life using the most meager of resources.

The earliest group we know much about are called the Norton people (because some of their artifacts have been found near Norton Sound along the Alaskan coast). They hurled stone-tipped harpoons at seals and other marine mammals from kayaks (light, maneuverable canoes made by stretching sealskins over a wooden framework).

The Dorset people (named after Cape Dorset) spread over much of Canada and Greenland beginning about 1000 BC. They, too, hunted seals as well as walrus and caribou. They lived in houses that were dug partly underground for warmth. The walls of turf and driftwood were covered on the inside with skins. Every house had an open hearth in the center of the floor and benches along the walls for the people to sit or sleep on. The Dorset also built skin tents, which were stretched tight over animal-bone frames.

> Have you noticed that most of the cultures you've learned about were named by people who lived long after they had disappeared? This is true with nearly all prehistoric peoples of the Americas. What did they call themselves? In nearly every case, they used a word that in their own language meant "the people."

The Aleuts settled along a long chain of islands stretching far into the Pacific from Alaska (known as the Aleutian Islands). The islands were kept relatively warm and perpetually rainy by the Japanese Current. (This was a current of warm water, similar to the Gulf Stream and the Humbolt Current.) The Aleuts fished in the Pacific and the island rivers, gathered shellfish and sea urchins along the shores, and speared octopuses among the rocks. Since the islands were never snow-covered, the settlers could usually find edible roots to supplement their diet of fish.

> The Aleuts cut seal intestines into strips and pieced them into their clothing. This made it waterproof!

Around 900 BC, a new culture emerged in northern Alaska. It gradually spread eastwards as far as Thule, Greenland (which is why it's known as the Thule culture). The Thule hunted seals, walrus, and even whales in skin-covered boats. Sometimes they chased caribou into wedge-shaped rock piles shaped like human figures (known as *inuksuit*). The frightened animals kept their distance from the rock figures until they ran into the point of the wedge, where they were trapped.

Thule hunters and fishermen made their weapons from bones, antlers, walrus ivory, animal sinews, and, of course, stone. They dressed in animal skins (the most valued one was that of the polar bear). They wore snow goggles carved from ivory. Narrow slits kept out all but a small part of the light, preventing snow blindness. (Modern skiers would never think of tackling a mountain on a bright day without goggles!)

The Thule built pit houses lined with boulders, whale skulls and bones, and sod. Whale ribs formed the roof rafters, which were covered with walrus skins and more sod. Raised flat slabs of rock served as sleeping platforms. Soapstone lamps with a moss wick burned seal oil for light, heat, and cooking. A house was entered through a long tunnel (up to 20 feet long) that sloped down and ended in a cold trap lower than the stone-paved floor. A visitor would climb up from the cold trap through a hole in the floor. The Thule came up with this practical design after discovering that cold air flows downward.

The Inuit

Among the descendants of these early Americans of the north were the Inuit, who lived in mainland Alaska, the Canadian Arctic, and western Greenland. The Inuit dealt so successfully with the challenges of the Arctic environment that their culture thrived basically unchanged for hundreds of generations. Even today, there are groups of Inuit living much as their distant ancestors once did. By studying the traditions and lifestyles of the Arctic dwellers of these "modern" Inuits and examining the artifacts recovered from the ancient past, we can learn quite a lot about how the first Inuit lived.

The word "Inuit" means *people* in the Inuit language. But they were called Eskimos by the Algonquian tribes of eastern Canada, and the Europeans explorers used that term, too. Eskimo means "eater of raw meat," which was not always the case with the Inuit. (They often cooked their meat over their oil lamps.) Even today many people mistakenly call the Inuit by the inaccurate Algonquian name.

First of all, we know that their year was organized around hunting. In winter, groups of families lived in one-room pit houses built of stone with rafters made of whalebones and roofs of turf. Like the dwellings of the Thule, the Inuit pit house was entered (on hands and knees) through a long subterranean passageway dug lower than the floor. Light from the outside came in the house through a hole cut in the wall, which was covered with a sheet of ice or pieces of seal intestine. A stone sleeping platform was constructed about 3 feet below the roof — the place where warm air collected. It was covered with fox and polar bear skins, and it was big enough for the whole family to stretch out on. The pit houses of the winter camp were often grouped around a larger structure, where the men had discussions and religious ceremonies took place. (This was the Inuit version of a kiva.)

The Inuit settlements were few and far between in that frozen wasteland. In fact, if the total population was distributed equally throughout the region they inhabited, there would be only one person per 250 square miles. This was no place for a city! Since the focus of their lives was on getting enough to eat, an Inuit band depended upon the leadership of the oldest and best hunter. Every family made its own tools and weapons.

A wife was an Inuit man's most prized possession, and wife-stealing was considered a major crime. It led to family vendettas that lasted for years. Children were doted upon, and the offspring of parents killed in accidents and illness (a frequent occurrence in the far north) were adopted by an older woman. She referred to the child as her "walking stick," hoping that she could lean on him, or her, when she was very old. But when food was scarce, a baby girl was the first to be sacrificed. (Girls were less valuable than boys because they would not grow up to become hunters.) A father made the decision that his baby girl must be killed for the benefit of the rest of the family, but the mother carried out the deed. Usually, she placed a caribou skin over the infant's face until she stopped breathing. Another method was to

> The Inuit and Aleuts looked much more like modern Southeast Asians than the earlier immigrants did. This is because of the appearance of their eyes. These later immigrants had fleshy eyelids and eyelid folds (giving the eyes an almond shape) to protect them against the sun — an adaptation that had not evolved in Southeast Asia when the first immigrants arrived in America. A modern descendant of the Inuit, placed in Tokyo, would resemble the people living there.

lay the infant in the entrance to the house, where she would freeze to death!

After they were comfortably settled in their winter quarters, the families (or, sometimes, only the men) packed their gear to hunt for seals, their main source of food, on the ice floes. During these expeditions, they lived in temporary shelters called igloos. (In certain regions of northern Canada, Inuit families spent the entire winter in an igloo.) An igloo (from the Inuit *igluviga*, meaning "home") was basically a dome fashioned from blocks of snow. To build one, an Inuit man first drew a large circle in the snow. Then he carved into the hard-packed snow within the circle with a knife made of a caribou antler. Working along the inner edge of the circle, he cut out rectangular blocks of snow and carefully placed them one upon the other in an ascending spiral until he had only a small hole at the top, which he left open for smoke to escape through.

As he worked, his wife plastered the outer walls of the igloo with fine, soft snow. The last step was to cut out a ventilation hole in the ceiling and a window in the wall, in which he inserted a sheet of clear, freshwater ice to admit light.

An Igloo

Like a pit house, an igloo was entered through a tunnel facing south and built low down, so that the wind was kept out and as little warmth as possible was lost from the family living space. The inside walls were covered with layers of fur and skins. A platform of packed snow several feet above the floor was used for eating and sleeping. Some light and warmth were provided by a soapstone seal oil lamp. The body heat of the family members added to the warmth, as did the natural insulation of the snow blocks themselves. In fact, the air could become warm enough for family members to shed their outer clothing. As ice on the inner walls melted, it formed a shiny glaze. It dripped down to the floor, where it refroze.

Hunting partnerships were formed at a very early age. When a baby boy was born, his mother made agreements with the mothers of 12 other male infants that their children would hunt together. Each boy was assigned a particular part of the seal. When the boys grew to manhood, they hunted seals as a team, and each was given his special part when an animal was butchered. (This tradition assured that every family had something to eat.) There were also song partners, usually two men who were good friends. Each would compose a song and teach it to his wife. Then, during a special festival held in the large meeting building, one wife would sing her husband's song, while he danced around, beating a drum. When they were done, the partner's wife would sing her husband's song, while he danced and played the drum. The songs were usually about hunting, but often they contained bits of humor, gently poking fun at the foibles of one another.

Seal hunting in winter took a lot of perseverance, since the animals spent most of their time beneath the surface of the ice. However, the seals had to breathe air several times an hour. They would scratch a number of holes through the ice as it began to freeze, periodically returning to them for air. As the sea ice thickened, a seal kept its breathing holes open, clearing away new ice as it formed. The hunters looked for these holes, often aided by their dogs. (When a dog sensed a hole, it would lie down at the spot.)

Once a breathing hole was found, the hunter would stand

beside it with a harpoon poised. He patiently watched for the quivering of the feather that was attached to a small, slender piece of whalebone stuck through the thin ice surface. The movement of the feather signaled the resurfacing of the seal. Given the number of holes, this could be a very long vigil.

Once he detected the movement, the hunter aimed and hurled his harpoon with all his strength at the surfacing seal. The harpoon head separated from the shaft as the seal was struck. The animal immediately dove back into the sea. A sealskin line about 30 feet long connected the harpoon head to the shaft so the hunter wouldn't lose his weapon or his prey. To anchor an animal after a hit, he might even plunge the shaft into the ice. When the wounded animal, hampered by the line, resurfaced to breathe, the hunter finished it off with a knife or lance. Hunters often drank the blood flowing from the seal's wound, then plugged it up with a carved piece of driftwood. (The blood was too precious to lose, as it was the major ingredient in "blood soup.")

> The Inuit language - Inukktitut - is not related to any other. Words and roots form complete thoughts. For example, igdlo means "a house," igdlorssuaq means "a large house," and igdlorssualiorpoq means "he builds a large house." So ideas are always linked to one word, whereas they would form a sentence or group of words in other languages.

At the end of the day, the hunters dragged the dead seals back to the igloos to be skinned and butchered by the women. The meat was often eaten raw by the family while it was still warm. Apparently it tasted good — and it provided valuable nutrients (although, of course, the ancient hunters had no knowledge of this.). The Inuit were especially fond of raw seal liver (a source of vitamins A and C). Some of the meat was simmered with blood and blubber over a seal-oil lamp, forming a thick broth. (This was the blood soup.) The remains of the carcass was left outside in a shallow pit, where it froze. Pieces of it could be hacked off and cooked at any time.

> Sometimes a hunter tied inflated animal bladder floats to their harpoon lines — the bladder kept the harpoon afloat if it missed the target so it could be easily retrieved.

Dogs were important allies of the Inuit. Their most important function was to pull sleds across the frozen terrain. The typical dogsled had two runners joined by crossbars. They were usually made from driftwood, but when this was not available the frame and runners were made of whalebone, ivory, caribou antlers, or baleen (a stiff hairlike material from the jaw of a whale). The runners were smeared with a mixture of earth and decayed vegetable matter, which was left to freeze solid. Then they were rubbed with a piece of fat, which enabled the sled to glide smoothly over the snow. In times of emergency, such as when a frame broke, the ingenious hunters made sled runners from frozen strips of seal meat!

It took six to twelve dogs to pull a loaded sled, the strongest dogs running in front. The leader was the smartest

An Inuit Sled Dog

(usually a female), which would respond to the spoken commands of its master. Harnesses were made of sealskin or caribou thongs. Sometimes, when the sleds were heavily laden with carcasses, the men and women had to help pull them.

Imagine how easy it was to get lost in the endless fields of white. Every direction looked about the same! An Inuit hunter learned to determine what lay ahead by "reading" the sky, which reflected the shades of the lands and sea below. When traveling across the sea ice, he knew he would reach open water where a dull gray cloud appeared on the horizon. On the other hand, a white glare in the sky ahead indicated that he had a large, snow-covered expanse of land to cross. He also looked for cairns (piles of stones set up by others to mark the way). Distances were measured not in miles but in "sleeps" — the number of nights required to reach a particular destination.

Inuit women collected "old" sea ice in sealskin bags. The old ice had lost much of its salt content and could be melted and used for drinking water.

In the late spring, when the ice began to melt and the sun rose higher above the horizon, groups of families left their winter quarters and traveled together to their summer camps, where they set up their skin tents. The women collected seagull eggs, roots, stems, berries, and driftwood. The men speared the wildfowl that had migrated north or entangled them with their bolas — three cords of plaited sinew knotted together with stones on the ends.

This was the time when fish swam upstream to spawn. The Inuit built weirs (net enclosures) in the rivers and streams or placed stone barriers from one bank to the other. Then they speared and netted the fish that became trapped.

> The Inuit calendar divided the year into 13 periods of 28 days each, according to the phases of the moon. Each month was named after what happened at that time, such as *Kahpidrah* ("it is cold) and *Hirkermaun* ("the sun returns"). *Voneve* was "when the baby seals are born."

Seals were now easy prey as they sunned themselves on the ice floes or gathered in rocky breeding grounds. The hunters harpooned them from kayaks or stalked them by crawling on their bellies across the floes. The Inuit kayak was an amazingly light and maneuverable boat. Its framework was made from animal rib bones or pieces of driftwood lashed together with sinew. This was covered with caribou hide, walrus hide, or sealskin, carefully stretched over the frame and sewn together. The craft was from 12 to 22 feet long and was totally enclosed except for a central cockpit, where the hunter sat. He wore a waterproof parka made of strips of seal intestines. The bottom of his parka was tied tightly to the rim of the kayak opening so that even if he flipped over, only his face and hands would get wet. He propelled the kayak with a double-bladed paddle.

A Kayak

Walrus were prime targets of the Inuit hunters, not only for their meat and blubber (they weighed as much as 2,000 pounds!) but more particularly for their teeth, bones, and ivory. These were essential materials for crafting tools and weapons as well as carving figurines. (The walrus meat was usually not eaten by the people but was fed to the dogs.) A walrus was easily harpooned on the rocky islands used as breeding grounds. To bring a carcass to shore, the hunters threaded lines through its skin and towed it, several kayaks working in tandem.

A Caribou

Throughout the summer, the Inuit hunted the caribou herds that migrated north. It was difficult to get close to the animals because the land was so flat and bare. Sometimes the hunters would sneak up on a herd, jump and down shrieking loudly to frighten the animals, and then chase them into specially built corridors of poles. Other times they killed small groups of caribou as they waded into the water at river crossings.

The Inuit used every part of the caribou they killed —the meat (for sustenance), skins (for clothing), antlers and bones (for tools), and sinews (for thread). Although some caribou roamed the snowfields in mid-winter, looking for any twigs that might be poking through the surface of the snow, they were rarely hunted at that time of year because their meat was too lean and their fur was too long and thick. However, if a family was low on food in winter, they would lure the caribou into pit traps by the smell of human urine — this attracted the animals because it was salty!

The Inuit fished in the open sea for cod and Arctic char, which they dried in the warm sun. But the real treasure of the deep was the whale. Hunting for a giant creature like a whale was extremely dangerous but worthwhile, since tons of meat and blubber could be harvested from a single animal. Whaling season began in late spring, when the bowhead whales migrated north. The whalers traveled in a *umiak*, a 30-foot-long open boat of driftwood covered with stretched walrus hide or sealskin. A single boat held up to ten men. (These boats were also used for transporting families to summer and winter camps.)

When a whale surfaced near a boat, a harpooner hurled his ivory-tipped weapon. The wounded whale dove quickly, pulling with it a line attached to the harpoon head. One end of the line was attached to floats made of inflated sealskins. Each time the whale came to surface, the hunters speared it with more harpoons. Finally, the exhausted animal gave up the struggle and was killed as a last thrust of a lance pierced its lung. The hunters towed the dead whale to shore where they butchered it, dividing it up into equal portions.

The summer diet was a varied one, a welcome change from all that meat. A favorite treat was the filled innards of certain birds and mammals, like the partly digested willow buds and twigs from the gizzards and intestines of ptarmigans (plump birds that roosted near the sea) and the seaweed from the innards of sea animals. A very special delicacy was seal intestines and stomachs stuffed with partly digested shrimp.

> The ptarmigan still lives in Alaska. It changes plumage with the seasons. In the summer its feathers are mottled, in the winter, white. Confident of its camouflage, the bird usually sits on its nest and calmly lets any predator approach. Sometimes it struts off to lure enemies from its eggs.
>
> In ancient times, both bird and eggs were easy targets for nomadic hunters!

As fall approached, the Inuit prepared stocks of dried meat and fish, which they buried in shallow pits so that they would have something to eat when they returned next season. The buried food would turn rather moldy and smell like old cheese when it was dug up, but it would provide nourishment until the new hunting season began. After making these preparations, the families set out for their pit houses at the winter camp. By August, the first persistent snows had arrived, and by September rivers and lakes were frozen. The long, dark winter had begun.

Daily Life of the Inuit

When a woman married, she took to her new home her two most prized possessions – her *ulu* (a crescent shaped bone or slate knife used for scraping hides as well as cutting leather and meat) and her sewing kit. She needed them because her major task, apart from caring for her children and preparing meals, was to make clothing for her family. Her needles were fashioned from ivory or the hard wing or leg bones of birds. Sinews from the caribou's back and legs made the best thread.

An Ulu

Most garments were made from the hides of caribou, which were both light and warm. The fur was left on. (The individual caribou hairs are hollow and each one traps body heat.) The best skins were taken in a fall hunt, when the hair was short. The women scraped and cleaned the skins with their ulus. Then they chewed and rubbed them until they were soft and pliable. They soaked some sinews in a small bowl of melted ice to soften and stretch them. Then they sewed pieces of hide together with a special tight "lock-stitch." As the wet sinews dried and shrank, the garment's seams became watertight.

It took twelve caribou skins to make a complete set of winter clothing for an adult: two pairs of pants and two parkas. Men and women wore both sets at the same time. The outer set was worn with the fur outside and the inner set with the fur next to the skin. Sometimes they wore underwear made from feathered duck skins. (Like the caribou hairs, the hollow feather quills held body heat.) Garments were made loose fitting so that air could circulate between the layers to provide insulation for added warmth. The hood of the outer parka was usually edged with wolverine fur (the only fur that didn't frost up from the moisture of the wearer's breath). The women's hoods were large, reaching to middle of their backs. Babies, dressed in suits of the finest fawn skins, were carried in their mother's hoods until they were two. (The babies wore diapers of soft, absorbent sphagnum moss.)

Mittens were fashioned from sealskin or (a luxury) polar bear fur. Warm waterproof boots were made from sealskin with soles of walrus or seal hide. The boots were often lined with moss or kelp to keep the insides dry. To protect their eyes, the Inuit wore snow goggles made of narrow pieces of wood or ivory. (Do you remember who first came up with this design?) The goggles fit close to the face above the cheekbones and under the eyebrows, and they were specially carved for every member of the family. The narrow slits permitted the wearer to see but reduced the sun's glare and prevented snow blindness.

> Some Inuit women fashioned bags from unusual materials, like fish heads. In the eastern Arctic they made coiled baskets from grasses, weaving strips of sealskin and whale sinew between the rows.

Sealskin clothing was preferred for rainy times and whale hunts because of its natural water-resistance. It was also more comfortable than caribou in the warmer weather.

Tattooing was considered a sign of a woman's eligibility for marriage. A young girl had her face tattooed with a series of parallel lines running from the center of her lip to the tip of her chin. This was done by an older woman in the family, who either pulled a soot-covered thread through the skin or pricked the skin with a needle dipped in a mixture of soot and seaweed. The girl was expected to endure this painful process without shedding a tear. Little girls had their noses pierced, so that beads could be hung there. A grown woman used the hole in her nose as a convenient place to carry her sewing needles!

The sign of manhood was a labret — a piece of ivory or even stone inserted in the skin at the corners of the mouth or under the lower lip. The lips were pierced in early childhood and small ivory pins were inserted. These were later replaced by ivory or stone studs of increasing size. A man might wear up to four labrets.

Most of the art of the Inuit had a practical function. Carving was a necessary skill, since bowls, tools, arrowheads and spearheads were always needed. Soapstone was ideal for making pots because it could take heat well. Damaged soapstone pots were mended with a cement made of blood, clay and dog hair. Then they were heated over a flame until the mend set. Ivory was used for carving items that needed to be strong, like harpoon heads and snow knives. Hunting records were sometimes kept by carving animal shapes or symbols on a piece of bone. This is the closest the Inuit ever came to a written language. They also carved animals from stone, bone, ivory, and driftwood. It was believed that the carving of these materials released an image that had been trapped within it. Recently, many tiny, delicate figures have been found that were carved thousands of years ago.

The life of the Inuit was certainly a demanding one, but they still found some time for leisure activities. During the long winter, families spent many hours indoors, To pass the time, they often played games, often ones involving gambling. (They made dice from bone.) One of the oldest games played all over the world, cat's cradle, was another favorite. A player wound a long cord of twisted sinew around the fingers of both hands to make shapes resembling animals and other objects of nature.

Everyone loves storytelling, and this is how the Inuit passed down the history of their families from generation to generation. It's also how they discovered explanations about some of the mysteries of the universe. As you might expect, the stories were filled with familiar animal characters of the Arctic, and they dealt with man's relation to the natural world. The storyteller recited the tales as dramatically as he could, often adding new episodes or insights of his own. Ivory "story knives," decorated with images of sea creatures, were used to sketch scenes from a tale in the icy floor of the igloo where the family was gathered. Many of the stories told by the earliest Inuit have been passed on for countless generations and are still heard, in widely varying versions, by people living in the Arctic today.

Religious Beliefs of the Inuit

For the Inuit, everything in nature — the animals, the sea, the heavenly bodies, the snow, even the earth itself — had a soul or spirit. All things were related, and so all things were sacred. There were many nature deities, such as the gods of the moon, sea, wind and snow. (The snow god appeared as a giant baby. Unfortunately, he hated people! Why do you think the Inuit thought of the snow in this way?) Stories were often told to explain happenings in the icy world of the Arctic. One described the frigid winds as the breath of a frost giant. Another described how winters came to be long and dark because a monster wolf swallowed the sun each fall.

Inuit religious beliefs centered upon the animals they hunted. One of the major deities was Sedna, a goddess who lived on the bottom of the sea and controlled the lives of the sea creatures. Sedna had a good reason to distrust human beings. According to an Inuit myth, she had been married to the Prince of Seagulls. But she was unhappy with him, and she called for her father to rescue her. He went to the land of the gulls, killed her husband, and fled in his umiak with Sedna. The gulls were so sad they began to cry in mourning (as they have ever since).

The gulls flapped their wings to create a terrible storm that threatened to swamp the boat. As the huge waves came crashing over the side, the father threw Sedna overboard. He hoped not only to lighten the load but also to appease the angry gulls. When she tried to climb back in, her father chopped off the first joints of her fingers! Her finger joints magically became whales when they fell into the sea. Still she held on, so he chopped away the second joints, which swam away as walruses. Then he cut off the stumps of her fingers, which turned into seals. Having no way to cling to the boat, Sedna sank downward into the bottom of the sea, where she became the sea spirit and mother of the sea beasts. Ever since, Sedna had taken her revenge by withholding the beasts of the sea from any human hunter foolish enough to offend her.

The Inuit considered it part of the natural cycle of life for animals to willingly sacrifice themselves so that they (the people) would have food and clothing. However, as the story of Sedna implies, the hunters were obligated to show proper respect for their prey and to never kill more than they needed to survive. To do otherwise would break the natural harmony of living things. The souls of the animals would become angry (as would Sedna), and they would no longer sacrifice themselves.

There were many ways to show respect for a slain animal. A hunter might place his harpoon beside an oil lamp the first night after a kill so that the animal's soul (believed to be still in the harpoon head) could warm itself by the flame. When a hunter brought a dead seal to his house, his wife covered the igloo floor with a layer of fresh snow. The animal was laid on its back on the snow, and the wife offered it a drink of water as a

All Inuits regarded themselves as equals. There can be no hierarchy or class society in a harsh environment where there is little margin for error. Each person has to be responsible for his or her own actions if he (she) is to survive.

Certainly, the men did work together as hunters and fishermen, but there were no laws as we know them. What worked best against the elements was what mattered above all else.

sign of hospitality. This guaranteed good hunting in the future, since the soul of the seal would report to other seals how well it had been treated. Then she distributed most of the meat to her husband's hunting partners. When a whale was killed, the head was severed, and the wife of the man that killed it offered it a drink of fresh water. This was intended to urge the whale's spirit to return to the sea to describe its good treatment so that other whales would return the following year. When a polar bear was killed, its skin was hung inside an igloo or pit house for five days, and presents were placed beside it to pacify its soul.

A fisherman would lay his catch in a circle around him with the heads of the fish pointing towards the water so that he would always be in the center of a school of fish. If seal hunters changed camps during the winter, they would arrange the skulls of the seals they had killed so that they faced in the direction of the new campsite. This enabled the souls of the dead seals to follow them and bring them good hunting.

Weapons were finely crafted not only for their effectiveness but also to please the spirit of the animal they killed. The spirit of a bird or seal that was slain by an ill-crafted weapon would carry the message to its kind in the spirit world and hunting would be bad. If, however, an animal was killed with a fine weapon, its spirit would be pleased and similar prey would be abundant.

At the beginning of the hunting season, festivals were held in which men wore animal masks to appeal to the animals and encourage them to return to be hunted. The Bladder Festival was held later in the hunting season. Many believed that the bladder of an animal contained its spirit and so, when an animal was killed, the hunter often carefully removed and preserved the bladder until it was time for the festival. Then, with great ceremony, the bladders were inflated (like balloons!) and hung in a special feast house. After much singing, dancing, and offering of food, the bladders were taken down and thrust into a hole cut in the ice. The spirits thus returned to the sea to enter the bodies of unborn animals, who would return to be hunted.

There were many taboos associated with the hunt. Land and sea animals could not be handled together in any way, since sea animals supposedly disliked coming in contact with those of the land. So eating caribou and seal meat on the same days was forbidden. Weapons that had been used for hunting land animals had to be smoked over a fire of seaweed before they could be used for killing a walrus. Clothing of caribou hides could not be sewn while seals, walruses, or whales were being hunted. Caribou meat could not be cooked over a fire of ocean driftwood. If these rules not observed, the animals would not allow themselves to be hunted.

The Inuit so admired certain animal qualities that they wore a variety of amulets (religious charms), such as owl claws to give them strong hands, caribou ears to ensure quick hearing, and a piece of polar bear bone to make its owner invisible when stalking the caribou, A fish skin was placed with a fisherman's tools to bring good luck, and a loon skin was sewn into the side of a kayak to give it good speed.

The most important person in the Inuit community was the shaman (SHAW man), who was believed to have mystical powers that allowed him to contact the spirit world. He alone could fight angry spirits, and it was his responsibility to discover the cause of poor hunting. The shaman could speak a sacred language handed down from the most ancient times, and he was entitled to wear a special headdress and belt. The Inuit depended upon him to cure sickness, which was believed to be caused either by breaking a taboo (through prayer, chants, and dramatic gestures, the shaman would seek forgiveness from the animal spirits) or by the loss of a person's soul (which the shaman tried to retrieve).

Every person had two souls. After his death, one of these would enter the body of a newborn relative, who would be given his name. It would guide the child throughout his life. If someone died of natural causes, his second soul traveled to the Narrow Land at the bottom of the sea. If he died violently, the second soul flew up to the Land of Day in the sky towards the dawn. In these two lands, the spirits of the dead lived much as they had done on earth, but without worry or care. The Land of Day life was especially festive, and the dancing lights of Aurora Borealis were said to be souls of the dead playing football with a walrus skull. There was also a third afterworld just below the surface of the earth. To this ugly place went the second souls of lazy hunters and women who could not endure the pain of tattooing. There was little to do there, and everyone was hungry. (The only food was butterflies!)

A dead body was wrapped in skins and laid on the floor of the family home. During the five days that the soul was believed to remain within the body, members of the dead person's family could do no work, and others in the camp could not comb their hair, cut their nails, or clean their lamps! Everyday life was in limbo. After the five days passed, the relatives placed the body on a sled and drove it far away from the camp. They laid it on the ice within a ring of stones, weapons and tools. Upon returning home, the family bathed themselves and thoroughly cleaned their homes. Those who had touched the corpse threw away the clothes they had worn and put on new ones. Can you see the reasoning for this? The people assumed the souls of the dead friend or family member had gone to another place, and that it was time for them to get back to the joys and challenges of everyday life.

THE SUBARCTIC WILDS

South of the Arctic tundra is a more diverse landscape of mountains, lakes, plains, and dense forests of spruce, birch, willow, and fir. This is the Subarctic. The vast forest region of the Subarctic is called the *taiga*. It stretches from southern Alaska across Canada to Labrador on the Atlantic coast. Although it can be as cold here as the frigid Arctic you've just be reading about, the trees offer some protection against the blasts of the wind. In ancient times, fur-bearing animals, like bears, foxes, muskrats, otters, beavers, and mink roamed the forest, as did moose and elk. Huge herds of caribou grazed on the nearby plains in winter, migrating north in summer.

For thousands of years, people survived in the taiga as nomadic hunters and gatherers. The forests offered not only shelter from the winds but an infinite supply of wood for building homes, making tools and weapons, and fueling fires to keep warm and cook meat. (What a difference the trees made! Think of how much easier it was to live in a forest, even a cold one, than in the barren stretches of the Arctic.) The trees also provided the material for boats. The tribesmen lashed together poles cut from white cedar with tough spruce roots to make frames for their canoes. They covered these sturdy frames with the bark of birch trees. In the warmer weather, they paddled the canoes through the lakes to catch the abundant fish and waterfowl.

A Birchbark Canoe

In winter, hunters stalked the caribou, which provided them with nearly everything they needed to live. They used the caribou hides for winter clothing — leggings, shirts, hooded parkas, mittens, and moccasins. and tent covers. Summer garb was the same minus the parkas and mittens, although some women wore leather skirts. But even in warm weather everyone covered himself (and herself) up completely as a protection against insects. (Remember those pesky mosquitoes that swarmed around the ponds and marshes of the tundra when the snow melted?) The Inuit also used caribou hide for their tent covers, and they twisted strips of leather to make snares for catching small game. The bones and antlers served as ax handles, fishhooks, and other useful tools. Of course, the tasty meat of the caribou provided the families with food. A special treat was the half-digested mass of lichens still in the stomach. It was roasted whole over a fire.

When not hunting the caribou in winter, the forest dwellers fished through holes in the river ice, scouted for hibernating bears, and dug out beavers from their lodges. And, like the people of the Great Plains, they relied for snacks (and for sustenance when the food supply was low) on a concoction similar to pemmican. They had made this in the fall by pounding dried caribou meat with fat and berries. They carried this mixture with them in birch-bark containers. (It lasted almost indefinitely.)

Toboggans (made from the same materials as those used for canoes) were used to carry heavy loads over the snow. They were usually hauled by the women, although they were sometimes pulled by teams of dogs. (Does it surprise you that the women had to haul the toboggans? In many Native American cultures, the men were charge of hunting, while the women did just about everything else! They considered it a fair exchange of labor. Do you?) Sometimes returning hunters used the quickly freezing carcass of the largest animal they had slain as a sled to slide the rest of their load of meat to their camp.

Like the Inuit, the women of the Subarctic often tattooed their faces. The men "spruced up" by wearing feathers in their hair and painting their faces with bright colors of paint made by crushed plants and minerals. Both genders wore necklaces and amulets made from bones, stones, and (if they lived near the coast) shells. Many pierced their noses to wear small trinkets there.

> They made snowshoes to track their prey by bending the thin branches of willow, spruce, or birch into loops and then lacing them with webbing fashioned from caribou leather. With this handy footwear, they could walk upon the deepest snowdrifts in the dead of winter.

Over the centuries, the inhabitants of the taiga formed two separate groups, who spoke very different languages. These were the Athabascan speakers to the west of Canada's Hudson Bay and the Algonquian speakers to the east. (Find Hudson Bay on the map on page 139.) Since the caribou lived primarily west of Hudson Bay, the eastern hunters pursued mostly smaller game.

The life of most Athabascan women was not particularly happy. A man in this culture group had several wives, and he might lose one at any time if he was beaten in a wrestling match by another man. When he lost a match, one of his wives was expected to move in with the victor without asking any questions. There are records of one woman who was lost and rewon by her husband seven times in a single day's wrestling!

The largest group of the Algonquian speakers were the Cree, who were divided into many widely separated bands. Like most early Americans, the Cree fashioned arrow heads, skin scrapers, and knives by flaking stones into sharp points. But their primary weapon was a bolo, made from stones tied together with strips of leather. A hunter twirled the bolo overhead, and upon its release, the rocks spun through the air and entwined the legs of his prey in the leather thongs. They weren't the only Native Americans to use the bolo, but they were masters of the art of throwing it.

Living in the dark forests could be frightening at times. There were so many shadows and mysterious sounds, particularly at night. The Cree worried about all kinds of unseen creatures, but most of all they feared giant monsters known as Windigos, who had an insatiable appetite for human flesh! Windigos were believed to be at least 30 feet tall and had bulging eyes, long pointed teeth, slavering lipless mouths, and hearts of ice. They began stalking the forest at the onset of winter, searching for human victims. If a hunter failed to return home, the inescapable fear was that he had been caught and eaten! A human could even turn into a Windigo if he was ever driven to eat human flesh to avoid starvation — something that often happened in winter. (When the migration routes of the caribou changed even slightly, many people had nothing else to eat.) And since a Windigo might disguise himself as a human hunter, any stranger who came to a village was viewed very suspiciously. No weapon could kill one of these monsters. Only the secret rituals of a powerful shaman would lay him to rest. (And, as in the stories of Dracula, a stake through the heart could destroy a Windigo!) Fortunately, the warm spring weather sent all Windigos fleeing north.

So much for monsters. Every early culture worried about some looming force within of darkness. (Do you?) But let's move on to more basic questions that puzzled the forest dwellers, such as the mystery of their own origins. The people of the Alaskan forests (the Athabascan speakers) handed down from generation to generation their own unique version of the creation of the earth. According to their belief, the world and everything in it was created by a magical black bird, the raven. Here's how it all happened.

This is a drawing of a Windigo by Bennett Wilson of Fay School. Since no one ever actually saw a Windigo, everyone's image of the monster is different. How do you envision this creature of the dark woods?

In the beginning, there was only darkness, but within the darkness was Raven. As he began to move along the dark ground, everything he trod upon sprang into being. It was a magical time. Water flowed from crevices and swelled to become streams and rivers, hills and mountains pushed up from below, and the trees of the forest came alive. This became the kingdom of the sky. But then Raven came to the edge of the land. Silently, he spread his wings and glided down through the darkness until he came to another land, which he called earth.

The raven is a large relative of the crow. It is a glossy, black bird, about 26 inches long. Ravens are strong, soaring flyers, sometimes performing aerial acrobatics. Their typical call is a croak, but they can utter other sounds as well and are able to mimic other birds. Ravens usually build their nests in cliffs and quarries, or sometimes in trees. They are usually scavengers, but they will attack small prey like rabbits.

Raven's presence brought life to earth and it, too, was soon covered with hills, streams, and forests. But it was still cast in darkness. Suddenly, Raven saw a tiny light coming from a fragment of mica, a shiny stone. As he scraped away the soil, the light grew brighter and brighter. Finally, he tossed the mica high in the air, and the earth was instantly flooded with brilliant sunlight.

Among the plants grew a giant pea vine, heavy with pale green pods. Suddenly, one of the pods burst open and out tumbled the first human being. Then Raven took a lump of clay from the river bank and molded it into two musk-oxen and two caribou. These beasts would provide humanity with food and clothing. Then he taught the man to make bows of wood and sinew and arrows tipped with bone to hunt the animals, but he cautioned him not to hunt too many. After making the other creatures of the forests — the birds, the fish, the beavers, the deer, and the others — he made a figure similar to man with a knot of fine grass for hair. This was the first woman. Finally, Raven taught man and woman all they needed to know to survive in the forests. More pods of the giant pea vine soon opened, and more people popped out. Raven taught them the same lessons.

The first people lived happily and had many children. For generations they followed the instructions of Raven. But one day, they became greedy and killed more animals than they needed. And they wouldn't even listen to Raven when he protested! The black bird was so disappointed that he abandoned the earth to return to the kingdom of the sky. But he couldn't forget about how the people had disappointed him. To punish them for their disobedience, he took the sun and wrapped it in a caribou skin bag. Now the earth was plunged in darkness. Raven finally took pity on the people and uncovered the sun for a day or two to allow some hunting, but then he hid it away again.

Raven married a young snow goose, and they had a son — Raven Boy. One day, while Raven dozed, Raven Boy crept to the chest where the caribou bag was stored and lifted it out. When Raven suddenly awoke, Raven Boy grabbed the bag and flew off into the darkness. Raven chased after his son, but he couldn't catch him. So he shouted to him not to hide the sun, but to let it shine on the earth sometimes.

Hearing these words, Raven Boy tore off the skin cover and set the sun back in place. The sunlight flooded the earth once again. Then, with a sweep of his wing, he sent the sky spinning around the earth, carrying the sun with it. Ever since, the earth has had daily cycles of darkness and light.

The people of the taiga led a hard life, although they didn't have to face the frozen conditions of their neighbors to the north. The winters were long, cold, and dark, and even in warm weather they had to protect themselves against the elements. But despite the hardships, many bands remained in this challenging environment. Others, however, moved further south, hoping to find a new home more to their liking. Some ended up in the Southwest. They are the ancestors of the Navajo and the Apache. Others moved into the Pacific Northwest, giving rise to such cultures as the Haida, Tlingit, and Kwakiutl. You'll learn about these cultures in Book II, but for now, let's find out more about the people who first settled along the Northwest Coast.

THE NORTHWEST COAST

When the nomads from Siberia first ventured across the land bridge, most of the Northwest Coast of America was covered by ice that reached to the edge of the ocean. But as the glaciers slowly melted, they left behind a 2,000 mile long ribbon of forested seacoast from the Gulf of Alaska to northern California.

A wall of volcanic mountains rose along the coast, the highest peaks cresting at more than 15,000 feet above sea level. In the far north, the mountains descended nearly to the sea, leaving only a narrow shoreline. Further south, from southern Alaska to Oregon, the coastal plain was wide, and here forested islands formed a protective barrier against the open sea, creating an inland waterway of fog-shrouded coves, bays, inlets, reefs, and marshes. The largest of the islands was Vancouver Island, sited just off the coast of Canada. Several major rivers sliced through the coastal mountains and cascaded into the sea.

The Northwest Coast had cool summers and mild, wet winters. Hard freezes were rare in all but the far north, since the ocean was warmed by the Japanese Current, and snow seldom covered the ground for long. The tall range of mountains blocked the continental cold to the east. The warm, damp air that was trapped between the sea and the mountains created an abundance of misty rain. (Today, rainfall can measure as much as 200 inches a year in the wettest sections of the coastal strip.)

Protected from the extremes of heat and cold, the sea along the Northwest Coast abounded with marine life. Kelp, a kind of seaweed, created an underwater thicket as dense as the tall grass of the prairie. The kelp attracted huge numbers of fish and other marine life, some of great size. The halibut weighed as much as 400 pounds. Alaska king crabs were bigger than most lobsters of today, and their legs were filled with succulent white meat — a tasty treat then as now. Cod and trout measured several feet from nose to tip of tale, and sturgeon were 18 feet long!

The tidal pools and shallows were filled with plankton, clams, mussels, crabs, sea urchins, and other small marine creatures. These provided meals for an assortment of seagoing mammals — sea otters, seals, sea lions — while whales and porpoises cruised offshore. In spring and summer, nearly every river along the coast was alive with fish heading upstream to spawn. Salmon as well as halibut, trout, cod, herring, and smelt made the rigorous trip against the fast-moving current. And during nesting season, thousands of seabird eggs littered the beaches.

A Grizzly

The mountain slopes rising beyond the narrow beaches were forested with towering spruce, hemlock, and cedar trees. Among these grew more than forty varieties of nuts and berries. The woodlands were inhabited by deer, elk, mountain goats, martens, beavers, skunks, and rabbits. Given the excellent hunting conditions, it's no surprise that many of the predators were of impressive size. Bald eagles grew large and strong on a diet of salmon, sea gulls (which ate just about anything) were as big as turkeys, and huge scavenging ravens dwarfed the gulls. Enormous black bears lived in the island forests, while giant grizzly bears roamed the mountain slopes and high meadows of the mainland.

The Northwest was not accessible to the first nomads journeying down the American continent from Beringia. Ice lingered at the higher elevations of the coastal range even after the land bridge flooded over, blocking an overland route to the Pacific Ocean. But by about 8500 BC, adventurous bands of tribesmen had traveled through the high, narrow passes carved in the mountains by swollen rivers and had entered the dense forests of Oregon and Washington. About five hundred years later, other groups began arriving by dugout canoe, carefully making their way down the coastal waters from Alaska.

Like the other immigrants we've learned about, the first people who ventured into the Northwest Coast made the most of their environment. Not that they had to work very hard. Dinner was there for the taking! They tracked the woodland animals with their stone pointed spears, and they fished with hooks made from the small bones of the animals they had slain. By 3000 BC, large numbers of people were gathering shellfish along the coast. They left behind huge mounds of discarded shells. (Remnants of these prehistoric dump sites still exist today.)

Nature provided plenty of raw materials for tools. For example, the large, rounded pebbles that washed up along the shores could be flaked on one end to a sharp point. These made useful knives that fit neatly in the palm of the hand. They were ideal for carving wood, skinning animals, and dressing fish. Some of the more creative newcomers carved beads and pendants from seashells.

Over the centuries, the population of the Northwest Coast grew. Many villages were established near the mouths of rivers. Few traces of these early villages have survived in the damp environment, where wood quickly crumbles and rots. However, there is enough evidence in the form of tools, building sites, and even human remains to provide a general picture of the cultures that existed as early as 500 BC. Also, artifacts that have been discovered from settlements established many centuries later indicate that the lifestyle of the coastal dwellers changed very little during all that time. Even in our own century, the descendants of the earliest settlers were living much as their ancestors had, and they provided even more clues about those ancient times.

The early settlers depended mostly upon seafood to furnish their food needs, and for good reason. Fishing the coastal waters was certainly much easier than tracking prey in the rough, forested terrain. And, as you know, the sea was rich with fish, crabs, and other marine creatures, many of which could be caught throughout the year. At first, the settlers simply speared any animals that swam or wiggled nearby. But in time, they learned to catch greater quantities of fish in the tidal zones by building stone enclosuress that were covered by water at high tide, permitting the fish to swim over them, only to be trapped when the tide fell. Some of the stone walls were over 100 feet long. The enclosures were carefully maintained over many generations.

When herring amassed to spawn, their numbers were so densely packed together that a fisherman with a herring rake (a pole with a row of bone teeth attached to it) could sweep up several fish at a time and drop them into his canoe. He would repeat the process over and over again. Branches were often placed below wooden buoys ini the sea to catch the much prized herring eggs.

A Salmon

But the main food resource was that leaping, silvery fish — the salmon. There were five species of Pacific salmon, all of which bore a rich, pinkish meat. The largest was the chinook salmon, which could measure five feet and weigh over 40 pounds. Salmon are born in mountain streams and rivers and then migrate to the sea. After about three years, they return to the place of their origin to reproduce. Beginning in late spring, the first huge runs of these fish moved inland along the Northwest coast, swarming over sandbars, battling river rapids, to spawn and then die by the thousands. In just a few months, a fisherman could catch enough migrating salmon to sustain his family for the rest of the year.

The easiest way to catch the salmon was to assemble lattice-like wooden weirs across the river to divert the fish from their upstream course while allowing the water to flow past. The weirs were similar to the stone enclosures built in the tidal zones. The trapped salmon were easily speared. For heavier fish, like the chinook salmon, the fishermen used bone-tipped harpoons with long shafts. Once the point penetrated the fish, it separated from its shaft. The man tugged on a line of sinew that was attached to the point to retrieve his catch. Nets made of nettle twine were used to scoop up smaller fish from the river.

Actually, there were so many salmon in the rivers, and their spring run was so predictable, that the early settlers came to regard these fish as deities. According to one of their sacred tales, a tribe of salmon people spent the winter in houses beneath the sea. When the air warmed, they changed into fish and swam upriver to offer their bodies to the humans. But their souls were immortal. So, after feasting upon a catch of tasty salmon, the people would always throw the bones back into the water to enable the soul of the fish to return to the sea. Otherwise, the salmon would not return the next season. (This, of course, is similar to the religious beliefs of the Inuit.)

Most of the salmon meat was preserved by drying it in the sun. The dried fish could later be pounded into fish meal, which could be kept for a long time to be used in soups, stews, or other dishes. The fish meal provided protein, and it thickened a broth when there was no fresh fish. It was also a handy food source to take along on hunting trips (like pemmican).

Although drying was the preferred method of preserving the salmon, the rainy climate of the coast often made it necessary to preserve the catch in smokehouses. Every village had a windowless structure in which the fish were hung from the rafters above a smoky central hearth. Even today, smoked salmon produced in thie way is a popular treat.

> History is filled with patterns. Here's one. Have you noticed how primitive people tend to deify (or consider sacred) whatever force or creature of the natural world provides them with food?
>
> Think about how important the rain god was to the ancient corn farmers, and you've just learned about Sedna, who provided the Inuit with sea animals.
>
> So it should come as no surprise that the early dwellers of the Northwest Coast should worship the salmon. It's only logical!

A tasty dish was made by aging some of the salmon roe (eggs). The roe was stored inside the stomach of a deer, which was then hung in a storehouse. The stomach was carefully kneaded from time to time as it dried (over a period of a few months) until eventually its contents turned into a cheese-like substance. This was considered a great delicacy!

The women learned how to extract oil from fish by boiling and then pressing them. Some of the oil came from the salmon, but the preferred fish was the eulachon, because it contained a larger amount of oil. (The eulachon was so full of oil that strings of the dried fish were often burned to provide a bright light at evening festivals!) The fish oil was stored in lined wooden boxes and in long tubes of hollow kelp, which were hung in the storehouses looped like a garden hose in a modern garage. The oil was used by the families for frying food. It was also traded to people living inland. The network of routes established to trade the oil were later known as "grease trails!"

In the spring, groups of men set out in huge dugout canoes to hunt whales. They rowed as far as twenty miles out to sea — well beyond the sight of land. Like the Inuit, the speared their quarry with harpoons and then towed it back to the beach, where they butchered it. The whale blubber was used for oil lamps, and, of course, the meat fed many people for a long, long time. The whale's huge intestines were cut into pieces and dried to made handy watertight containers for food. Its sinews were braided into ropes, and its bones were fashioned into tools.

> Off the coast of Vancouver Island, killer whales would often scratch themselves on the large rocks. Local legends arose to explain that the whales did this so that they could turn into wolves, their terrestrial counterparts. Then they could search for food in the thick forests the same way they did in the water.

The dense forest provided the early settlers with plenty of wood. The red cedar is a tall and majestic evergreen tree that grew in abundance along the coast in those early times. Cedar is a beautiful hard wood that has a very pleasant aroma. (Moths, however, hate the scent, so modern people often line their closets with cedar!) The wood is also resistant to rot, a big plus in a rainy place like the Northwest Coast. The cedar provided the early settlers with so many products that they came to think of it as a generous spirit of nature that, like the salmon, longed to serve them.

A cedar could be felled in a fairly short time by a team of men using stone adzes. (An adze was a heavy, curved stone blade, ground and polished to a fine edge, that was attached to a wooden handle.) One of the main uses of cedar timber was the construction of homes. The coastal dwellers lived in large rectangular buildings, each of which housed several families. Massive logs formed the framework of a house. Wide planks of split wood formed the outer walls. The planks were grooved or notched so that they could be joined together without the use of pegs. (Metal nails, of course, were unknown.) The houses were usually built along the beach of a sheltered bay, with their doorways facing the ocean. The

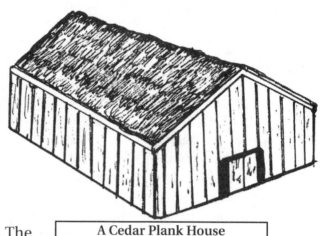

A Cedar Plank House

average house was 30 feet wide and 60 feet long. Many were more than double that size! In some cases, an entire village might live in a row of houses built closely together that extended for up to 1,000 feet.

Despite their size, the plank houses were transportable. When the villagers moved to another site for seasonal hunting or fishing, they took down the planks and carried them with them. When they got to their second site, the refitted the planks on the foundations they had dug in previous years. And when it was time to return to the coast, they carried the planks back and reinstalled them in the foundations beside the sea.

Cedar logs were also fashioned into canoes. A log was hollowed out by stoking a smoldering fire within it. The fire softened the wood, which could then be scooped out with adzes. Then the boat builders stretched the log into canoe shape by filling it with heated water, which again softened the wood. Canoes came in many sizes. The smaller ones were used to travel along streams and small rivers. Larger ones were used for fishing and whaling. Canoes as long as 60 feet were used for trade and warfare. They held a crew of 50, who energetically paddled for hundreds of miles from their coastal villages.

The cedar was also carved into boxes. These were used to store practically everything — dried fish and meat, fish oil, cords of animal sinew, ceremonial garments, and parts of weapons. A box was often made from a single cedar plank, with deep grooves scored across its surface. The plank was steamed to make it pliable, then bent at the grooves to form a box with seamless corners. The top consisted of another plank, which had been notched around the edges for a snug fit. Wooden pegs were driven into carefully drilled holes to secure the box, and all joints were sealed with a clamshell paste to make it watertight. The cedar boxes were often elaborately carved, using a beaver-tooth knife or chisel. Sometimes they were painted with figures of humans and animals as well as geometric patterns.

Even clothing was made from cedar. The women pounded the tough fibers of cedar bark with a stone until it was softened and then cut it into strips. These could be woven into cloth. Split cedar root was woven into mats for covering the walls and floors of houses and into baskets with a mesh so tight they could hold water. Finely woven cedar-root also proved ideal for foul weather gear —

Hat, Cloak, and Skirt Made from Cedar Fibers

capes and broad-brimmed hats of woven cedar provided a water-proof shield against the frequent rains. Cedar fibers were even twined into ropes, fishlines, and nets. Like the corn of Mesoamerica, the cedar tree was the wonder plant of the Northwest!

The leaders of the early settlements were the heads of their clans. Next in line of power were their sons, younger brothers, and other close relatives. Most of the community was made up of ordinary people; who had little political power. But even here there was a hierarchy — canoe makers were held in higher esteem than simple fisherman. Slaves made up the lowest rung of coastal society. These were the women or children who had been taken in raids against other villages. (Men captured in battle were usually killed.)

For "dressup," young women wore flakes of mica on their faces, an ancient form of glitter! And young men greased their skin with bear fat to make it look shiny. Both men and women wore ear and nose pendants. In the northern regions, the men also wore wooden or bone plugs through their lower lips.

Families selected wild animals as their totems. There were the Salmon People, the Beaver People, the Bear People, the Killer Whale People, and so on. Each group believed that their special animal had helped their ancestors. They carved figures of their totem creature on wooden poles of (that's right!) cedar. This is the origin of the famous totem poles associated with this region.

Over the centuries, certain families gained control of the best fishing grounds, berry patches, and cedar groves. As the rights to these assets passed from one generation to the next, a more complex social hierarchy developed that was very different from that of most ancient cultures in North America. The wealthy competed among themselves to prove who was richer! Special ceremonies were held in which wealthy families doled out their surplus goods to the common people living in their town or village. Then they stood back and waited for compliments about their generosity! This was probably the origin of the spectacular "potlatch ceremonies" that were staged by prominent members of various coastal tribes in later years. We'll learn more about these ceremonies as well as totem poles in Book II.

From a Totem Pole

The coastal dwellers told many tales about the spirits of the sky and sea and about the creatures that became their totems. A key character was the Trickster-Creator known as Raven (the same bird described in the origin myths of the Subarctic). Most likely, many stories traveled with the people during those early migrations from the north. But despite a wealth of stories, the people of the Northwest Coast never developed an organized religious tradition anything like those of the Mound Builders or the Mesoamericans. They had no regular religious ceremonies and built no temples (as far as we know). As with other groups that depended upon hunting for their survival, the main function of their shamans was to make certain that the animals were treated with respect so that others would allow themselves to be hunted.

And yet, the combined treasures of the sea and the forest gave rise to a way of life unique in prehistoric America. Without ever having to resort to taming the land or growing crops, the coastal dwellers lived quite comfortably. Don't you think?

REVIEW QUESTIONS

1. What is permafrost, and how does it determine the type of vegetation in the Arctic?
2. Name six animals that live in the Arctic.
3. What groups are considered ancestors of the Inuit?
4. How were hunting partnerships arranged by the Inuit?
5. What were the basic steps involved in hunting seals?
6. Describe an Inuit dogsled and team.
7. Why did the Inuit hunt walrus?
8. Why was the caribou hunted?
9. What were an Inuit woman's two most important possessions?
10. Who was Sedna and why was she worshipped?
11. What religious ceremonies were held by the Inuit before a hunt?
12. What did the Inuit do with their dead?
13. How is the Subarctic different than the Arctic?
14. What were the two major groups of the taiga?
15. Why was the Windigo feared?
16. According to the people of the taiga, what animal created the first people?
17. Describe the geography of the Northwest Coast.
18. What was the main source of food in the Pacific Northwest?
19. What were the uses of the cedar tree?
20. What were some of the totems of the coastal dwellers?

PROJECTS

1. The Vikings were the first Europeans to contact the Arctic dwellers in the 10th century. They visited Thule settlements in Greenland and northeastern Canada as early as the tenth century AD. The Vikings referred to the natives as Skraelings, their word for savages. This should give you a hint about how they treated the Americans. Archaeologists have found evidence of their settlement at L'Anse Aux Meadows in Newfoundland, Canada. Find out more about the Viking settlement and their relationship with the natives. Then write a short report describing your findings.

2. Poet Ogden Nash wrote a whimsical poem about the windigo of the northern woods. It's entitled "The Wendigo." (There are two spellings.) Find it in your library and read it to your class. Below is how Jesse Schacht of Fay School envisions a windigo. Draw your own version of this man-eating monster.

3. Find out more about the modern Inuit. Write a report, comparing their lifestyle with that of their ancestors.

4. Did you know that the dog has been "man's best friend" for more than 140,000 years? DNA evidence shows that dogs evolved from their wolf ancestors at just about the same time that early humans first left Africa. Find out more about the evolution of the dog from the wolf and of the dog's history with humanity. Write a short report stating your findings.

GLANCING BACK

Whew! In just six chapters you've covered thousands of years of history! Isn't it amazing how many wonderful things were accomplished in America before it was "discovered" by European explorers? How could anyone call this a "New World?"

Before concluding this part of the story of the first Americans, let's take a moment to glance back at some of the central themes. You'll see some interesting patterns, which will help you understand how early cultures were formed in many other places throughout the world.

First and foremost, there's the challenge of the natural environment. Imagine yourself suddenly dropped in the wild without the benefits of modern technology, supermarkets, and shopping malls. How would you survive? You'd have to use whatever materials you could find to serve your most basic needs — food and shelter. Suppose the ground was covered with ice and snow, as in the Arctic. Then you'd have to depend upon any animals you could catch for everything, just as the Inuit did. What if you were in the scorching desert? Rocks and caves might be the best solution for shelter, and you wouldn't be fussy about what you ate — roots and insects are delicious when you're very hungry! Of course, some environments, such as the eastern woodlands of North America, are more people-friendly. But even there, you'd have to be pretty imaginative and resourceful to make your tools and weapons from stones, sticks, and animal parts. Along the Northwest Coast there are plenty of fish to eat, but how would you cope with all that rain? And what about the sweltering rainforests of Brazil and the lowlands of Mesoamerica, where the ground is covered with vines, and towering trees block out the sunlight?

Okay. Let's say you've learned to survive in the wild. Now how about making your life a little easier? Once again, you'd have to be pretty inventive. But let's not dismiss the element of luck. The early Americans often made some world-shattering discoveries by accident — remember how they learned to plant seeds? But most of the time they had to experiment — this involved lots of trial and error — until they figured out how to do things like channel water or design a sturdy structure. So would you.

Could you survive alone? Probably not. But by working with your friends and relatives, you might be able to obtain an adequate supply of food for long periods of time. The earliest Americans certainly knew the importance of teamwork. And once they learned to farm, cooperation took on a whole new dimension. Remember how it went? The farmers grew enough crops for the community, while others concentrated on what they did best — everything from making pots to ditch-digging.

Suppose you lived in a prehistoric settlement. Wouldn't you be scared of natural occurrences like thunder storms and earthquakes? This is where the nature gods came in handy. If you could assume that *they'd* take care of running the universe as long as you expressed your appreciation (through prayers, ceremonies, and personal sacrifices), wouldn't you feel more comfortable about the mysteries of life? And living so close to nature, you'd notice many things that modern people take for granted. Like the stars and planets, for example. Looking at the heavens every night, you might observe that certain bright objects move in particular ways that become, over time, almost predictable. It would be nice to keep track of the changing patterns, wouldn't it? But how? Maybe by cutting some marks on a piece of wood, or drawing a picture on a stone wall with a small chunk of colored mineral rock... You know what's coming next, don't you? Of course! This is how some thoughtful ancient Americans took the first steps toward creating a system of writing.

Are you beginning to have a better understanding of the challenges faced by the first Americans? Good! Remember this: whenever you want to understand history better, put yourself in the time and place of the people you're studying. Imagination is one of the best learning tools!

But the story's only partly told. In Book II you'll read about the descendants of "the ancient ones." Huge numbers of people were thriving on the American continents at the moment of "impact" — the arrival of European explorers and settlers that would bring an end to life as they knew it. Wouldn't you like to learn about the mighty Inca of South America, the bloodthirsty Aztecs of Mexico, the practical Sioux of the Great Plains, the democratic Iroquois of the Eastern Woodlands, the peaceful Hopi of the Southwest, and the boastful Kwakiutl of the Northwest Coast — to name only a few? Then on with the story!

TIMELINE

NORTH AMERICA (north of Mexico)	MESOAMERICA	SOUTH AMERICA
30,000-20,000 BC—Siberian hunters cross Beringia **12,000 BC** — Beringia floods over **9,500 BC** — Clovis culture flourishing **9,000 BC** — Folsom culture flourishing **8,000 BC** — Plano culture flourishing **1,500 BC** — farming in Southwest; Poverty Point **1,000 BC** — Dorset culture begins to spread over eastern Arctic **900 BC** — Thule culture beginning **900 BC -100 BC** Adena culture **500 BC** — fishing villages in northwest **300 BC** — Hohokam, Mogollon, and Anasazi well established **100 BC - 400 AD** — Hopewell **100 AD** — Inuit well established **300-1000 AD** — Hohokam **500 AD** — Mimbres Valley culture **700 -1200 AD** — Mississippians **900-1100 AD** — Chaco Canyon **1000 AD** — Viking settlement in Newfoundland **1200 AD** — Cahokia at height **1300-1400 AD** — Mesa Verde **1450 AD** — Decline of Cahokia	**5,500 BC** — First crops in Mexico **5,000** — First corn in Mexico **1,200 BC** — Olmecs get started, San Lorenzo founded **900 BC** — La Venta founded **150-750 AD** — Teotihuacan **200-900 AD** — Maya at their peak **500-1000 AD** — Tiahuanaco thrives **950 AD** — Tula founded **1200-1300 AD** — Chichen Itza	**10,000 BC** — People arrive at the tip of South America **7,000 BC** — Farming in the mountains of Peru **700-200 BC** — Paracas culture **500 BC** — Chavin de Huantar at its peak **200 BC** — Nazca culture **200-700 AD** — Moche culture

Note: These dates are approximate!

INDEX